OUTSPOKEN

OUTSPOKEN

Series editors: Adrian Parr and Santiago Zabala

Pointed, engaging, and unafraid of controversy, books in this series articulate the intellectual stakes of pressing cultural, social, environmental, economic, and political issues that unsettle today's world. Outspoken books are disruptive: they shake things up, change how we think, and make a difference. The Outspoken series seeks above all originality of perspective, approach, and thought. It encourages the identification of novel and unexpected topics or new and transformative approaches to inescapable questions, whether written from within established disciplines or from viewpoints beyond disciplinary boundaries. Each book brings theoretical inquiry into a reciprocally revealing encounter with material realities and lived experience. This series tackles the complex challenges faced by societies the world over, rethinking politics, justice, and social change in the twenty-first century.

Outspoken

A Manifesto for the Twenty-First Century

EDITED BY ADRIAN PARR
AND SANTIAGO ZABALA

McGill-Queen's University Press
· Montreal & Kingston · London · Chicago

© McGill-Queen's University Press 2023

ISBN 978-0-2280-1692-2 (cloth)
ISBN 978-0-2280-1693-9 (paper)
ISBN 978-0-2280-1821-6 (ePDF)
ISBN 978-0-2280-1822-3 (ePUB)

Legal deposit second quarter 2023
Bibliothèque nationale du Québec

Printed in Canada on acid-free paper that is 100% ancient forest free
(100% post-consumer recycled), processed chlorine free

Library and Archives Canada Cataloguing in Publication

Title: Outspoken: a manifesto for the twenty-first century / edited by Adrian Parr and Santiago Zabala.

Names: Parr, Adrian, editor. | Zabala, Santiago, 1975- editor.

Series: Outspoken (McGill-Queen's University Press)

Description: Series statement: Outspoken | Includes bibliographical references and index.

Identifiers: Canadiana (print) 20220474850 | Canadiana (ebook) 20220474931 | ISBN 9780228016922 (cloth) | ISBN 9780228016939 (paper) | ISBN 9780228018223 (ePUB) | ISBN 9780228018216 (ePDF)

Subjects: LCSH: Social action. | LCSH: Political participation. | LCSH: Social problems.

Classification: LCC HN18.3 .O98 2023 | DDC 306—dc23

This book was typeset by Marquis Interscript in 10.5/13 Sabon.

Contents

Figures

OUTSPOKEN

Introduction

Adrian Parr and Santiago Zabala

WHY DO WE HAVE TO BE OUTSPOKEN IN 2023? HOW DID WE GET HERE?

It is 2006 and Tarana Burke releases the phrase #MeToo on Myspace, a social network platform, to raise awareness of sexual violence. With its simplicity and clarity, the hashtag goes viral when actress Alyssa Milano tweets it in 2017, calling out the powerful Hollywood film producer and sex predator Harvey Weinstein. Weinstein is later convicted of sexual assault. #MeToo goes on to become the platform for a global movement for the survivors of sexual harassment and assault, and for those who advocate against these crimes.

It is 2013 and George Zimmerman, a Neighborhood Watch member, has just been acquitted for fatally shooting seventeen-year-old Trayvon Martin as the highschool junior walked to his father's fiancée's home at Twin Lakes, Sanford, Florida. Like many young Black people who have suffered a similar fate, Martin was unarmed. Tired of the repeated murders of Black people at the hands of law enforcement, three Black women – Alicia Garza, Patrisse Cullors, and Opal (Ayọ) Tometi – ignite a social justice movement with the release of their hashtag #BlackLivesMatter. The Black Lives Matter activist movement shines a spotlight on racist violence in the United States, prompting thousands to take to the streets in protest. Black Lives Matter demands that the police be defunded and the savings diverted to marginalized communities. With each killing of an unarmed Black person – witness Michael Brown (2014), Eric Garner (2014), Tamir Rice (2014), Laquan McDonald (2014), Sandra Bland (2015), Freddie Gray (2015), Terence Crutcher (2016), Alton Sterling (2016), Deborah Danner (2016),

Antwon Rose (2018), Atatiana Jefferson (2019), Breonna Taylor (2020), and George Floyd (2020) – the Black Lives Matter movement renews its demands for the overhaul of policing policies, the defunding of the police, and the diversion of public money to support marginalized communities. In less than a decade the #BLM hashtag grows from being a protest rallying cry with local chapters across the United States to being an internationally influential anti-racist social justice movement.

It is 2018 and the international Youth Strike for Climate movement begins with a simple gesture repeated once a week: fifteen-year-old Greta Thunberg skips school every Friday to stand quietly outside the Swedish parliament holding a sign that reads *Skolstrejk for Klimatet* ("School Strike for Climate"). This uncomplicated lone action of a vegan schoolgirl diagnosed with Asperger's syndrome sparks an international youth climate justice movement. It galvanizes hundreds of thousands of children around the world to join her in school strikes against climate change and to campaign hard for prompt and meaningful action.

All three movements began with one clear idea that set off a series of tangible actions against injustice. Each of them was an outspoken response to a perceived emergency. All were designed to unravel systems of power and privilege that discriminate, harm, and oppress underprivileged groups. The intermeshing of these systems highlights the way in which environmental and social justice issues feed on each other. Indeed, their very imbrication – and our blindness to it – constitutes the biggest emergency humanity has ever faced.

* * *

Now, a mere two decades into the twenty-first century, the social and environmental emergencies that people are encountering the world over are reaching epic proportions. It is time to put the brakes on the dumping of human waste into the earth's atmosphere, land, and waterways. It is time to turn around a global economic system that centralizes wealth in the hands of a few and results in massive inequities that have forced millions into abject poverty and bankrupted entire nations. The time has come to end the sacrificial zones of refugee camps, the prison industrial complex, the CO_2–laden skies, the destruction of other-than-human habitats. It is not enough to recognize that the climate is changing, that ecosystems are collapsing; without concrete and meaningful action, disinformation abounds and species extinction continues unabated.

While any number of directly experienced emergencies occur daily – flash-flooding, wildfires, growing houselessness, scarcity, surging white supremacism, growing numbers of refugees – one of the greatest emergencies that life on earth must grapple with is more opaque and structural in nature. The greatest emergency is the absence of a sense of emergency. Normalizing capital accumulation and militarism has let loose an oppressive, discriminatory, and intolerant sociality. As the editors of this volume, we understand that in this context unspokenness has the potential to destabilize the gap between systemic and individual instances of violence; it can interrupt, interrogate, and ultimately destabilize violent modes of social organization.

What makes violence structural is the way it works, and in the twenty-first century it works through displacement and slippage. A prime example is the way British Petroleum responded to the 2010 Deepwater Horizon oil spill that allowed 210 million gallons of crude oil to gush into the waters off the Gulf Coast. The company simply turned the disaster into a rebranding opportunity – "Beyond Petroleum" – all the while continuing to invest in fossil fuels. This slippery slope – publicly announcing an intent to move away from an International Oil Corporation (IOC) to an Integrated Energy Corporation (IEC) at the same time as lobbying the US administration for drilling rights in the fragile Arctic – is not only disingenuous; it epitomizes the insidious ways in which structural violence operates. Violence in the twenty-first century is becoming increasingly difficult to nail down, to neatly identify and circumscribe, and accordingly be called out for what it is. That is the greatest emergency *Homo sapiens* faces.

Being outspoken in our current context might begin simply by reactivating the human imagination, starting to envision alternatives that are more inclusive, compassionate, generous, and equitable. Galvanizing the imagination in this way could empower a speaking out against the authority that today's *modus operandi* of violence holds over the human imagination – an authority that derives from its way of stripping the futurity out of the future. For the exercise of imagination is itself ultimately conditioned by futurity; it draws its productive and creative potential from an immanent reality, albeit a reality to come, which so far remains unrealized. As an imaginative undertaking, outspokenness is a political modality, in that it situates being within the future-oriented coordinates of the present.

In today's circumstances, being outspoken is both an act and a concept of plasticity, a mode of doing politics and an event that is constituted collectively and in turn unleashes spheres of solidarity; it is a directive and an aspiration; a way of being and a means of co-creating knowledge – both an ontology and an epistemology.

Outspokenness, as it is tackled throughout this book, is a mode of affirmation, a differentiating force that both sustains and makes room for difference. It is contingent, in that it changes over space and time; and it is through this state of contingency that the political promise of being outspoken arises because it means being less vulnerable to appropriation. It is resistant to being integrated into the market because as it moves it is not easily co-opted and turned into another function of the free market. As such, it contains within it the possibility for authentic emancipation from the ruthlessness that drives life under global capitalism.

* * *

In the constellation of essays that make up this volume, each brings its own distinctive take on how being outspoken works in our contemporary world; but in their respective ways they also have a philosophical resonance with each other. We have organized the synergies that have emerged across the anthology into three sections. Part One constitutes an effort to define our outspoken age; Part Two gives voice to various artistic, social, political, and economic engagements with being outspoken; and Part Three examines how an outspoken politics might work. Although we recommend that readers begin with the first two chapters, which set the tone for the anthology, the individual chapters do not necessarily need to be read in the order they are presented.

Henry Giroux's and Katerina Kolozova's contributions offer key interpretive insights into how to critically examine the current social and political climate. Giroux's demonstration of how Trump effects are more significant than any policies Donald Trump enacted, as they will "surely outlast Trump's retreat," leads into Kolozova's distinction between the illiberalism of the ethno-nationalist right and the anti-liberalism of the radical left, widening our focus from Trump and American politics and culture in particular. The contributions of Eduardo Mendieta, Francesco Pallante, and Michael Loadenthal respond to three different issues – the power of constitutionalism, the flaws of direct democracy, and the role of the anti-fascist today – issues that together are connected to questions raised by Giroux and Kolozova.

The essays of Thaïsa Way and Amelia Jones set the tone for Part Two as they explore different ways of "being outspoken" through the arts, activism, and speech acts. Thinking about the future of design, Way highlights the important "contributions to spatial justice and democracy" that designers provide, and makes a cogent appeal to support this essential work. The "soul of a strong democracy," she maintains, lies not only within the realm of institutionalized politics; the built environment is also "foundational to democracy." Jones makes a similar distinction between "art as activism" and the "arts as programming." While Way "reinforces the neoliberal late-capitalist structures of power," Jones advocates for using a "broader and a more appropriately performative concept" rather than a "global" art audience as a means through which to mobilize communities. These distinctions are also developed in the essays of Cleo Davis, Kayin Talton, Alex Taek-Gwang Lee, and Natasha Lennard, which together offer readers different collectivist paradigms of political mobilization.

Contributions by Rosi Braidotti, Chiara Bottici, Jennifer Grubbs, and Slavoj Žižek make up the closing section of the book. Articulating a concept of "negative toxicity," Braidotti describes a misogynistic pulse driving life in the contemporary world which finds expression through masculine rage, sexual violence, and transphobia. In this context, being outspoken constitutes a posthumanist feminism geared to support "the formation of a heterogeneous subject who forcefully argues that, yes, 'we-are-in-this-together-but-we-are-not-one-and-the-same.'" Bottici and Grubbs build upon on Braidotti's insights, proposing an "anarcha-feminism" and "rebellious mothering" for the future. Meanwhile, Žižek enquires whether there is a "third way" outside the extremes of populism and institutionalism. He concludes by turning to Greta Thunberg – a model for outspokenness – as a source for a reimagined communism built on the realization that "doing our best is no longer good enough."

If the volume's contributions run across many different disciplines and perspectives, it is not because they lack coherence; rather, as "being outspoken" implies, it is intrinsically a singular process that operates by differentiation. As we can see, being outspoken is hermeneutical; it demands and requires all the help it can get in these times of political, social, and ecological crisis. Although the ancient concept of *parrhesia* or "frank and fearless speech" – as Michel Foucault's late lectures showed – has always been central to the critical function of philosophy and its political vocation, today there is a demand to intensify our outspokenness.

Now more than ever there is much to speak up and out about; yet, what exactly does being outspoken mean in the twenty-first century? How does it work? What is its transformative potential? Is it an intervention into the normative operation of the social field? Does it consist of a refusal to participate, or is it a form of engaged citizenship that works to transform the system from within? The contributions that follow, when considered together, suggest that being outspoken is a little of both. It is at once radical and reformist. It inaugurates a moment when you, or I – or we – no longer accept the displacement activities that divert our attention from the emergency shaping and informing our everyday lives. It is an affective happening of public exposure, an artistic instantiation that invokes another subject, space, and time by breaking free from the designated and politically sanctioned sites of social activity and expression. It is a mode of breaking free; it is taking up a burning flag – such as John Gerrard has pictured on this book's cover – and running with it.

PART ONE

Outspoken Age

Trumpism and Its Afterlife

Henry A. Giroux

The storming of the Capitol in Washington, DC, on 6 January 2021 by a mob of neo-Nazis, white supremacists, and other right-wing extremists, incited by then US president Donald Trump and his discourse of hate and violence, provided a clear example that the United States no longer lives in the shadow of authoritarianism; it had tipped over into the abyss. Trump was not alone in creating a pretext for such violence. Prior to the assault on the Capitol, the right-wing media, especially "Parler, Twitter, TikTok and the pro-Trump message board The Donald," posted messages incessantly "calling for violence – including the arrest and execution of politicians."[1] Stoking the crowd's sense of resentment and thirst for destruction, Trump repeated his delusional belief that the election had been rigged, urged his supporters to march to the Capitol, and told the unruly gathering: "You'll never take back our country with weakness. You have to show strength."[2]

His incendiary rhetoric of lies and calls for retaliation were exacerbated by Republican politicians who actively promoted conspiracy theories and dangerous propaganda in order to invalidate the election of Joseph Biden. Some of them appeared at the rally just before the invasion of the Capitol and used inflammatory language to further incite the crowd. Rudy Giuliani, Trump's discredited lawyer, for instance, told the protesters: "If we're wrong, we will be made fools of. But if we're right, a lot of them will go to jail. So, let's have trial by combat."[3] US Senator Josh Hawley, in a shameful display of political opportunism, greeted the crowd with a raised fist as they marched on the Capitol.

Under Trump's administration, lies, ignorance, and a thirst for violence had taken an increasingly lethal direction. It had moved from violence waged against immigrants, Black and brown people, and the poor to the violence of a right-wing mob attacking the police, rampaging through the Capitol, and occupying the House and Senate chambers. Not only did Trump advertise a call for a demonstration among his supporters but he also brought to the event a history of encouraging them to express themselves through violent means.[4]

What the president and the mob shared was a hatred of democracy, however fragile, and the discredited belief that the election was stolen. In the aftermath of the assault, he sent out a series of tweets supporting the actions of the mob, after which he was rapidly suspended from Twitter.[5] At the same time, the domestic terrorism that took place on 6 January was about more than Trump's lies and his use of language in the service of violence.[6] It was also about a new political formation called Trumpism, with its mix of white supremacy, voter suppression, market fundamentalism, and authoritarianism.

Trumpism represents a new form of fascism in which older elements of a fascist past are recycled, modified, and updated. One example can be seen in the systemic lying of the sort that was both at the heart of Hitler's regime and central to Trump's rise to power and the development of his social base, though the latter expressed itself in a different context and through a unique set of cultural apparatuses. Historian Timothy Snyder is instructive on this issue:

> Post-truth is pre-fascism, and Trump [was] our post-truth president. When we give up on truth, we concede power to those with the wealth and charisma to create spectacle in its place. Without agreement about some basic facts, citizens cannot form the civil society that would allow them to defend themselves. If we lose the institutions that produce facts that are pertinent to us, then we tend to wallow in attractive abstractions and fictions. Truth defends itself particularly poorly when there is not very much of it around, and the era of Trump [was] one of the decline of local news. Social media is no substitute: It supercharges the mental habits by which we seek emotional stimulation and comfort, which means losing the distinction between what feels true and what actually is true.[7]

In the current wave of Republican Party politics with its persistent lies about the election, ongoing attacks on critical forms of education (including the banning of books), curtailment of women's reproductive rights, and intensified onslaught on civil rights, it is clear that Trumpism will be with us well into the next decade. As free-speech activist Samuel

Farber has observed, "the conditions that gave rise to his brand of noxious politics aren't going away anytime soon."[8] Trading on a politics of resentment, an economy of decline, Trump's ability to conceal his links with big capital, and his alleged image as an outsider, Trumpism has emerged as a "political mood and state of mind, and … movement" with a social base that "is more likely to endure than Trump himself."[9] Kenny Stancil, a writer for *Common Dreams*, points out that one sign of the indiscriminate loyalty of Trump's base was that: "Among Republican voters, 45% approve of the storming of Capitol, 30% think the perpetrators are 'patriots,' 52% think Biden is at least partly to blame for it, and 85% think it would be inappropriate to remove Trump from office after this."[10]

Trump's diverse mob of neo-Nazis and white supremacists, along with the conditions for the attack on the Capitol, had been building for years in the dark recesses of conspiracy theories, lies, white rage, backlash to the Civil Rights and Black Power movements of the sixties, and a hatred of those critics considered "enemies of the people."[11] President-elect Biden called it an insurrection, making it clear that Trump, through his language of denial and incitement, had fanned the flames, particularly in the speech he gave before the mob stormed the Capitol building. This was Trumpism in full bloom, with its ignorance, hatred, and penchant for lawlessness on full display. But it was more: it testified to the notion that fascism begins with language and ends with violence. The mob violence aimed at shutting down the counting of electoral ballots was reminiscent of the brutality of the thugs who roamed the streets of Germany in the 1930s silencing dissenters and those considered "other" in the deranged Nazi notion of racial and political cleansing. Trump unleashed his fascist impulses consistently through the language of violence and divisiveness, aided by right-wing media such as Fox News, Breitbart, and others. Under the Trump administration, ignorance turned lethal. Moreover, as scholar of critical race theory David Theo Goldberg has commented, "politics today is nothing short of a civil war" marked by divisions and disunity in which life for a sizable number of people in the United States has become both unbearable and dangerous.[12]

This is not surprising, given Trump's post-march statement of affection ("We love you") and allegiance to the extremists who marched on the Capitol. More specifically, Trumpism is the culmination of a cultural and fascist politics that has been evolving and intensifying for years through the incitement of lies, conspiracy theories, and the heated rhetoric of racism and war on the welfare state and working-class people.[13] The acts of domestic terrorism in the storming of the Capitol reach far beyond the toxic personal politics, incompetence, and corruption of Trump himself. Such violence has a long history in the United States, and under the aegis of Trumpism it has been normalized as a right-wing populist movement, which Trump brought to the surface of American politics as a badge of honour. What is necessary to comprehend is that violence in Washington, DC, did not begin with the 6 January march; it erupted in 2016 when Trump seized upon and manipulated the fears of powerless whites and white supremacists who imagined themselves as under siege and oppressed outsiders. For four years, he incited violence through attempts to inspire and energize his white-supremacist and fascist followers.

Every era produces language and cultural markers that offer insight into its politics, its values, and its vision of the past, present, and future. This is especially true of the economic, public, and cultural influence of the Trump presidency and mode of governance. Trumpism goes beyond the personal behaviour of Donald Trump. It refers less to a person than to a dangerous movement and social base, and operates as a social pathology whose endpoint is the destruction of democracy itself. As a new cultural and political construct, Trumpism merges a ruthless capitalist rationality, widening inequality, and a commitment to white supremacy. These forces have deep historical roots in the United States. What is distinctiveunder the Trump regime, however, is that they have congealed into a unique political and cultural formation marked by an emotively charged, spectacularized, and updated form of authoritarianism that echoes elements of a fascist past. In the current historical moment, Trumpism has intensified and quickened the dark forces of hate, racism, ultra-nationalism, and white supremacy.

At the same time, Trump merged the mobilizing passions of an updated fascist politics with the financial institutions and regressive values of a cruel and savage capitalism in order to undermine democratic institutions and values. Trump's presidency was rooted in the long-standing history of economic inequality, racial injustice, nativism, and war on the social state, while Trumpism as a social movement emerged from the shadows of history, revealing fascist elements that moved from the margins to the centres of power.

* * *

At the heart of Trumpism is a shocking political and ideological system of repression. It was created by a hateful, heartless, and pathologically lying president who, as activist journalist Masha Gessen argues, "taught Americans that no one will take care of us, our parents, and our children, because our lives are worthless, disposable … that this country is a dangerous place [and that] we are forever on the brink of disaster and that no one will protect us, whether from illness or economic hardship."[14] Trumpism has intensified this culture of fear through a variety of tools of repression – ranging from mass incarceration, surveillance, and police brutality to a full-fledged attack on those who would bring reality into play and hold power accountable – to enforce a worldview in which lawlessness and political corruption have become the order of the day.

Trumpism is an ongoing historical and political interlude dominated by a language of forgetting, moral irresponsibility, and the spectacle of cruelty and violence. In the oft-quoted words of the Italian marxist Antonio Gramsci, one might say that Trumpism occupies the interregnum between "the old world [which] is dying, and [a] new world [struggling] to be born." Trumpism is the in-between or third space between the old and the new in which "a great variety of morbid symptoms appear." While it is not clear what is being born, it is obvious that the struggle between the forces of authoritarianism and new modes of collective resistance has taken on a new urgency. The symptoms of Gramsci's "time of monsters" are upon us. This was especially true as Trump was about to leave office, in that he defended the legacy of the Confederacy, spewed lies about the legitimacy of a free and fair presidential election (which he had lost), pardoned war criminals, corrupt politicians, loyalists and personal friends, and threatened to use martial law to force a new election.[15]

As journalist Jennifer Evans observed at the time, Trump may have lost the election, "but Trumpism is alive and well, along with the conditions that propelled him to power in the first place. At best, the post-election future might be one of regrouping and rebuilding; at worst, there will be more challenges to legal norms and truths by the outgoing president and the Republican Party."[16] As the enemy of democracy, Trumpism is a mix of a capacious authoritarian ideology, a right-wing propaganda machine, and a fascist ethos. Its power and influence far exceed Trump's presidency, and it will not end with Biden's. In its afterlife, it will continue to sabotage democracy in the name of minority rule, its only endpoint the tyranny of

authoritarianism. As an anti-democratic ethos, it has opened a political chasm in which any attempt to unify the nation seems almost
unachievable. Trump's relentless politics of divisiveness is a toxic
platform for inciting violence, affirming a culture of cruelty, and promoting a politics of exclusion and racial cleansing.

Trump's ongoing penchant for violence was clear in his urging his
followers to engage in "wild" protests when they gathered in
Washington, DC, on the day Congress was due to certify President-
elect Biden's electoral college victory.[17] His extremist supporters,
like the Proud Boys, not only need someone to blame for their seething resentment of immigrants and Black and brown people; they also
value violence as the only available cathartic remedy to offer any
sense of resolve, emotional relief, or gratification. There is more at
work here than a long-standing assault on truth, reality, and democracy. There is also an embrace of the more dangerous elements of a
fascist politics with its regressive authoritarian impulses and its
espousal of politics as an extension of war, and violence as the ultimate register of a battle in which there are only winners and losers.
Trumpism makes clear that the forces of barbarism are no longer
hiding in the dark; if they are to be resisted we need a new language,
a renewed politics, and a sense of collective struggle.

Trumpism is a cancer whose roots have long infected the body poli-
tic. In the current age of brutality, it symbolizes governance without
empathy or compassion. It is widely acknowledged that this aspect of
Trumpism was responsible for the deafening silence that met the
shocking and unnecessary deaths of hundreds of thousands infected
by COVID-19[18] – a silence all the more appalling since those deaths
were largely due to the bungling of an administration that chose conspiracy theories over science, replaced the authority of public health
officials with the opinions of incompetents, and lied about the severity
of a virus that spread through the population like wildfire. National
leadership vanished, both with respect to controlling the spread of the
virus and organizing the vaccination campaign.

As a death-dealing form of cultural politics, Trumpism further
removed the government from any sense of social responsibility, raising apathy, cruelty, and moral indifference to a central mode of
governance. In another example, Trump and his sycophants and cult
followers remained shockingly silent in the face of the murder of
Heather Heyer, a young counterprotester killed in a Charlottesville
Unite the Right rally. In addition, indifferent to human suffering,

spurred on by his white-supremacist senior speech writer Stephen Miller, Trump imposed unjust travel bans, enacted cruel deportation laws, and engineered the separation and caging of migrant children who, according to a detailed report by Americans for Immigrant Justice, experienced conditions described as "inhumane" and "horrific."[19]

Trump's election and presidency made clear not only that authoritarianism was once more on the march, but also that a new and revised form of fascist politics had emerged in the United States, mimicking a pattern seen abroad. Of course, the seeds for this updated model of authoritarianism had long been germinating, especially since the 1970s, under capitalism, with its marriage of money and politics and its tendency to make corruption and inequality instruments of control. Under Trump, the merging of power and repression became glaringly visible, given his claim to unchecked power and flagrant acts of lawlessness.

Under Trump, power, repression, and corruption were mobilized increasingly in the political and cultural spheres both to shape public consciousness and to undermine, if not destroy, any institution that held authority to a measure of accountability. Trumpism redefined corrupt power relations, flagrantly displayed immoral and criminogenic behaviour, and unabashedly brandished the trappings of tyranny. As Gessen further writes in describing Trump's presidency:

> In plain view, Trump was flaunting, ignoring, and destroying all institutions of accountability. In plain view, he was degrading political speech. In plain view, he was using his office to enrich himself. In plain view, he was courting dictator after dictator. In plain view, he was promoting xenophobic conspiracy theories, now claiming that millions of immigrants voting illegally had cost him the popular vote; now insisting, repeatedly, that Obama had had him wiretapped. All of this, though plainly visible, was unfathomable, as Trump's election itself had been.[20]

Trumpism enacts a form of power on steroids. It aims to capture institutions of the state not only for personal and political gain but also as a means of redefining and controlling language, social media, and popular culture so as to empty politics of any substance, turning it into a spectacle. Under the banner of Trumpism, language operates in the service of violence, and all forms of criticism are relegated to the category of fake news, unworthy of serious reflection or critical analysis. At its core it is a cultural politics that shreds any viable notion of shared values or national unity, reducing essential human connections to bonds of distrust and fear. It views the space of the social, the common good, and democratic values as a zone of weakness and resentment bristling with hatred if not a seething logic of disposability.

Trumpism, however debated, has acquired an identity as a distinct new political formation, increasingly signifying an amalgam of power, culture, politics, and everyday life that combines the harshest elements of a cut-throat global capitalism with the lingering malignancy of neo-fascist forces that ranged from "white supremacist, white nationalists, militia, and neo-Nazis and Klans, to the Oath Keepers, the Patriot Movement, Christian fundamentalists, and anti-immigrant vigilante groups."[21] Molded in the language of populist, racist, and authoritarian nationalism, Trump's reign gave birth to a tsunami of repressive political, economic, and social policies that moved from the margins of society to the White House and to state and local governments around the country. Voter suppression and border terrorism were embraced as legitimate policy measures. As the social state came under severe attack, the punitive state grew, with its ongoing militarization of civil society and its increasing criminalization of social problems. Children of undocumented immigrants were put in cages, walls rose up as a normalizing symbol of nativism, and state terrorism came to define the role of Immigration and Customs Enforcement, becoming visible in the use of military forces to attack peaceful demonstrators in cities such as Portland and Washington, DC. War, dehumanization, divisiveness, hate, and the language of racial cleansing and sorting became central governing principles and set the stage for the rebirth of fascist politics.

Trumpism reached into every niche of civil and political society, cross-pollinating politics, culture, and everyday life with a range of right-wing policies, authoritarian impulses, and emerging right-wing movements. Right-wing militia patrolled the southern border of the United States; authoritarian forms of parliamentary state governments, wrapped in the mantle of democratic elections, waged wars on people of colour through voter suppression laws; and the Republican Party, mobilized by an unmitigated hatred of democracy and support for minority government, became the political arm of Trumpism, embracing the dictates of white nationalism, white supremacy, and an unapologetic right-wing version of American exceptionalism.

Increasingly, near the end of Trump's term, party members voiced attempts to overthrow an American election on the basis of bogus conspiracy theories and no evidence of fraud – attempts that in some cases resembled sedition.[22] The possibility that the president and his enablers may have committed a seditious act was all the more resonant in light of their direct and indirect support of the actions of the mob storming the Capitol. This was the view that president-elect Biden appeared to support in a speech given in the aftermath of the "failed insurrection" when he stated that such lawless action "borders on sedition."[23] The violence, racism, bigotry, and lawlessness that marked the assault on the Capitol represent the new face of a politics inhabited by "genuine fanatics and ideologues" who, in their blind loyalty to Trump and their own thirst for power, demonstrate that "cowardice is contagious."[24]

*** *** ***

On one level, one could say that Trumpism emerged out of a crisis in transnational neoliberalism, which can no longer lay claim to democratic values while concentrating wealth and power in the hands of the ruling class, accelerating wars and an unprecedented degree of economic inequality worldwide. While many critics have defined Trumpism in terms of its debasing, toxic language, and cruel policies – all of which are important issues – few have analyzed it as a pedagogical practice whose impact on political culture has redefined and reshaped the collective consciousness of the millions who embraced it more as a cult than as an ideology fabricated in lies, false promises, and authoritarian populism.[25] Trump's egregious bungling of the COVID-19 crisis, which cost the lives of over 300,000 by the end of 2020, his "disdain for immigrants, for women, for disabled people, for people of color, for Muslims – for anyone who isn't an able-bodied white straight American born male," and his blunt embrace of ignorance have had lethal consequences. Yet, his actions have done little to undermine his base of support.[26] In mobilizing the support of over 74 million Americans, Trumpism made clear that changing consciousness through his use of social media and right-wing cultural apparatuses was more persuasive politically and ideologically than the use of military force.

What this suggests is that politics follows culture, and that winning the struggle for the hearts and minds of people is the first step in creating the social base to support a fascist politics in which justice dies, language loses its moral and critical bearings, and the right to lie becomes a virtue. Massive inequality has made the struggle to survive a central component of everyday life for millions of Americans. In this instance, what is at risk is not just the ability to fulfill basic needs, but the very nature of one's identity, dignity, and sense of agency. Trumpism created a culture that induced a moral and political blackout, legitimated by a sycophantic, Vichy-like Republican Party, and normalized by a right-wing corporate-controlled mainstream social media. Trumpism is a giant pedagogical disinformation machine whose aim is to colonize culture and public consciousness, and undermine any viable form of robust and critical modes of agency, identification, and solidarity.

As a pedagogical tool and cultural force Trumpism is designed to reshape the public sphere by emptying it of democratic values and destroying the institutions that nurture critical thought and civic courage. How else to explain Trump's reactionary call for a "patriotic" curriculum, and his disdain for the New York Times "1619" education project, which aimed to place the consequences of slavery and the achievements of Black Americans at the centre of the American national narrative?[27] One could also point to his concerted effort to destroy public education with the appointment of Betsy DeVos, a publicly acknowledged sworn enemy of public schooling and higher education.[28] Unsurprisingly, the New York Times editorial board described DeVos as "perhaps the most disastrous leader in the Education Department's history."[29]

Under Trump, the centrality of education to politics became obvious with the growing use of twenty-first-century cultural apparatuses such as Twitter, Facebook, and Google, along with new media outlets such as Fox News, Newsmax, and Breitbart. These pedagogical apparatuses have produced a distinctive cultural space that furthers the marriage of power and civic illiteracy, and works to erase the crucial question of what civic education and literacy should accomplish in a democracy.[30] Favouring instant reactions and a culture of immediacy, the new-media and new image-based cultural forms have turned chaos, catastrophe, and collapse into a spectacle that offers instant gratification, along with a kind of "digital sublime" in which such platforms are "mythologized as both convenient and infallible."[31] Flooding the media ecosphere with lies, misrepresentations, and dangerous if not deadly falsehoods, these new cultural-pedagogical apparatuses package hate and undermine the critical role of intellectuals, journalists, experts, and other voices working on the side of truth, evidence, and meaningful authority.[32] Regardless of design, one outcome has been to undermine and weaken traditional markers of freedom of expression and democracy.

Trumpism performs politics as a form of entertainment and digital drama. It does so by transforming the political realm into a form of spectacularized theatre, not unlike what Guy Debord once called *The Society of the Spectacle*.[33] As a right-wing cultural apparatus, spectacle of disintegration, and tribal ethos, Trumpian politics becomes an all-encompassing tool of propaganda using a pedagogy of repression and functioning as a form of cultural politics under the control of a corporate elite. As a reactionary cultural and pedagogical conduit, Trumpism undermines critical dialogue, shared values, shared responsibilities, and informed judgments, while promoting authoritarian narratives that disdain historical consciousness, critical thinking, and the principles of participatory democracy. In alignment with authoritarians such as Hungarian leader Viktor Orbán, Trumpism views democracy as something to be scorned. Its embrace of white Christian nationalism, racial cleansing, and anti-immigrant ideology evinces a deep hatred of liberal democracy with its notions of self-development and the self-determination for all citizens, enabled by access to relations of equality and power. Hard boundaries, nativism, precarity, a culture of fear, untrammelled individualism, an all-encompassing ethos of self-help, and a profound unease make up the currency of Trumpism. Economic justice, meaningful solidarities, and the common good are removed from the discourse of politics and citizenship.

* * *

There is more. Trumpism enacts, without apology, a form of historical amnesia that proves particularly dangerous in a world wrought with anxiety and uncertainty, and in the precarious present moment enveloped by pandemics and plagues. Falling victim to a politics of erasure by government and corporate disinformation machines, historical consciousness loses its sense of critique, its context, and its memories of the value of individual and collective resistance in the face of systemic oppression. Historical vision, moral witnessing, and democratic ideals are obscured by a glut of misinformation, lost in a spectacle of political corruption, a plague of consumerism, a culture of immediacy. Bombarding the cultural and public spheres daily with provocative and explosive news, Trumpism produces a relentless tsunami of events that crowd out the space and time for contemplating the past, while freezing the present in a fragmented display of shock and spectacle.

Under such circumstances, the lessons of history are lost, along with evidence of similarities between an authoritarian past and an authoritarian present. One consequence is that public consciousness of the need for critical reflection withers, as well as an understanding of the past as a source of critical insight. History, with its dangerous memories, it is said, cannot be repeated in the present – especially not in a country that makes a claim to exceptionalism and therefore argues that Trump's behaviour is more performative than dangerous. In this discourse, the dark shadows of an updated fascist politics are hidden behind the claim that Trump is merely incompetent and that his politics are inept and bear no resemblance to those of an incipient dictator.[34] Conservatives who believe that the market is the only template for politics and governance refuse to see Trump's rule as an outgrowth of their own disdain for the welfare state and the redistribution of wealth and power, while liberals live in fear of recognizing that it is neoliberal capitalism that poses the greatest threat to democracy and creates the conditions for the ongoing threat of fascism.[35]

This view serves as a breeding ground for liberals who argue that Trumpism is a passing and failed anti-democratic exception to the rule. The historical record needs to be revisited, for instance, regarding the liberal view of Trumpism especially evident in the work of Samuel Moyn, who argues that traditional institutional checks proved successful against Trumpism. He also claims – falsely – that Trump provided a "portal for all comers to search for alternatives beyond [neoliberalism], and never provided a systemic threat to American democracy."[36] Moyn's notion that Trump was anti-militarist and a champion of the working class, at least initially, rings especially false. Not only did Trump give the financial elite a \$1.5 trillion tax break in lieu of funding crucial social programs; he also passed policies that promoted what Saharra Griffin and Malkie Wall, researchers at the Center for American Progress Action Fund, call corporate wage theft. These policies included derailing "an Obama-era plan to extend overtime protections to more Americans," with the result that salary thresholds were lowered and "workers [were] denied an estimated \$1.2 billion in earnings annually due to Trump's overtime protection rollback."[37] Trumpism made it difficult for workers to unionize while making it easier for employers to eliminate unions. This anti-worker campaign also included reducing workplace safety regulations, discriminating against people with disabilities, and weakening civil rights protections for workers.

What is overlooked in this view is that Trumpism enacts the end-point of the historical failure of capitalism, which has morphed into a nihilistic death drive – a quickened call to ugliness, violence, and dehumanization – reinforced by market values that destroy all sense of moral and social responsibility.[38] According to John Bellamy Foster's *Trump in the White House: Tragedy and Farce*, Trumpism is not simply about Trump the bungling leader, a decrepit Republican Party, or a weak president, as Moyn, Jeet Heer, Cass Sunstein, Ross Douthat, and others have argued. Also missing in this view's politics of denial is an honest look at the emergence of Trump's undisguised authoritarian impulses – as are the mobilizing elements of a fascist politics that is an extension of capitalism and whose recent endpoint emerged with the violent assault on the Capitol – and on democracy itself.[39] Trumpism may not constitute a fully formed fascist regime but, as Sarah Churchwell, Timothy Snyder, Paul Street, and Jason Stanley have argued, the Trump regime has consistently embraced the long-standing and malignant traditions of American fascism.[40] Snyder dismisses the liberal claim, most recently advanced by Third Reich historian Richard Evans, that the fascist label does not apply to Trump because his ideology and policies do not invite a direct comparison.[41] Snyder writes:

These last four years, scholars have discussed the legitimacy and value of invoking fascism in reference to Trumpian propaganda. One comfortable position has been to label any such effort as a direct comparison and then to treat such comparisons as taboo. More productively, the philosopher Jason Stanley has treated fascism as a phenomenon, as a series of patterns that can be observed not only in interwar Europe but beyond it. My own view is that greater knowledge of the past, fascist or otherwise, allows us to notice and conceptualize elements of the present that we might otherwise disregard and to think more broadly about future possibilities.[42]

Scholars such as Moyn, Sunstein, and Corey Robin engage in a politics of denial, refusing to look honestly at key elements of fascism that Trumpism has mobilized. These include: flooding America with lies and launching a full-fledged attack on truth and science; enacting racist fear-mongering and a politics of disposability; promoting extreme nationalism and celebrating an alignment with dictators; endorsing a discourse of winners, along with a list of losers and enemies who became objects of contempt, if not violence; labelling the American press the "enemy of the people"; legitimizing a culture of cruelty and dehumanization that normalized, among other morally depraved acts, putting children in detention camps; reinforcing the language of misogyny and xenophobia; and using a powerful rightwing propaganda machine to legitimize a culture of lawlessness and political corruption.

What is missed by these centrist liberals, who often parade as leftists, is that Trumpism is the unapologetic face of neoliberal capitalism that induces massive inequalities, manufactured ignorance, and appalling degrees of hardship and suffering among diverse groups of people who are rendered excess. It concentrates wealth and power in the hands of a financial elite. Moreover, it is the logical outcome of a savage neoliberal capitalism that colonizes subjectivity in order to turn people into isolated consumers and atomized individuals willing to suspend their sense of agency and consider all social bonds to be untrustworthy. In this discourse, fate is solely a matter of individual responsibility, irrespective of wider structural forces. Abandoned is what Tony Judt, the late historian of postwar Europe, called "the thick mesh of mutual obligations and social responsibilities" to be found in any substantive democracy.[43] The logical outcome of this thinning of social connections that serve the common good is an individual and collective need for the comfort of strongmen – a default community that offers the swindle of fulfillment. Trumpism is a worldview in which critical thought collapses into what psycho-historian Robert Jay Lifton calls "ideological totalism."[44] Under the influence of ideological totalism, says Lifton, narratives of certainty are produced through a language frozen in the assumption that there is "nothing less than absolute truth and equally absolute virtue," all of which provides the conditions for "sealed off communities."[45]

Frank Bruni, an opinion-writer for the *New York Times*, asks just how rotten Trump would need to be for his followers to wake up and realize what a threat he is to democracy and their very lives. In raising this question, Bruni puts into high relief the cult-like and mind-boggling submission and irrationality that shapes the consciousness of many of Trump's followers. He writes:

Trump was impeached. A plague struck. Tens of millions of Americans lost their jobs and huge chunks of their savings. Trump responded with tantrums, lies and intensified attacks on democratic traditions. Trump's supporters reinvented or decided to ignore his coronavirus denialism, which made America a world leader in reported infections and recorded deaths and has had catastrophic economic consequences. They disbelieved or forgave all of his cheating: on his taxes, in his philanthropy, when he tried to extort the president of Ukraine, when he grabbed another Supreme Court seat in defiance of the Merrick Garland precedent. They accepted or outright embraced his racism and nativism. They shrugged off his lying, which is obvious even through the pore-minimizing filters of Fox News and Rush Limbaugh. They endorsed his cruelty and made peace with his tantrums and erratic behavior.[46]

Activist Coco Das goes further, arguing that America has a Nazi problem that will not go away on its own and must be addressed. Das observes:

We have a Nazi problem in this country. Some 73 million people voted for it ... They don't, for the most part, wave swastikas and salute Hitler, but we have a Nazi problem in this country as deeply as the German people had a Nazi problem in the 1930s. Their minds waterlogged with conspiracy theories, they take lies as truth, spread hate and bigotry, wrap themselves in several flags – American, Confederate, Blue Lives Matter – and use the Bible as a weapon of violence and repression. They are a grotesque expression of the worst of this country, of its ugly narcissism, its thuggish militarism, its ignorance ... They carry the torch of slavery, genocide, and Jim Crow terror. Gunned up and mask-less, they exalt above all the right to kill.[47]

* * *

In light of the refusal to view seriously the emergence of an updated fascism under Trumpism, a more comprehensive critical analysis of Trumpism is needed. Such an approach should offer insights into the blind allegiance of Trump's followers and the legacy of an authoritarian malignancy – white supremacy among others – that has resurfaced in American political culture. One necessary insight is the recognition that any understanding of Trumpism as a version of authoritarianism carries with it elements of a fascist past that can easily disappear into a discourse in which historical similarities are dismissed. Robin, for example, goes so far as to claim that Trump was a weak leader marked by political incompetence, who failed in his attempt to change the political culture.[48] This wild misreading of Trumpism goes hand in hand with the charge that those who claim Trump has resurrected the mobilizing passions of fascism represent what David Klion called "unhinged reactions to the Trump era."[49]

It is difficult to take such a charge seriously in light of a range of policies enacted under the Trump regime that are as cruel as they are oppressive. These range from voter suppression and the unleashing of the military on peaceful protesters to savagely cruel anti-immigration policies and a politics of disposability that, as Richard A. Etlin reminds us, mimics the Nazi policy of "'Vernichtung lebensunwerten Lebens,' that is, the 'destruction' or 'extermination' of 'lives not worth living.'"[50] The effect that Trump has had on political culture in the United States is far more significant than the policies he enacted. The real damage and corrosive impact produced under the Trump regime is the assault on ethics, the rule of law, the normalization of white supremacy, the blatant disregard for truth, evidence, and science. Trump legitimized a culture and pedagogy of hate, dehumanization, uncertainty, and authoritarian nationalism. These forces will surely outlast Trump's retreat to Mar-a-Lago, his Palm Beach estate.

Moyn, Robin, and others make no acknowledgment of the centrality and the power of the cultural politics and neoliberal and authoritarian pedagogies at work under Trumpism and how they "get people to give up their ideas of freedom and civility [while] giving them a taste for savagery."[51] Moreover, to dismiss critics on the left who describe authoritarian, if not fascist elements in Trumpism as unhinged is an egregious example of bad faith. Michael Yates responds to such derogatory attacks on left critics of fascism, buttressed by the alleged whitewashing of the danger Trumpism poses. Focusing on Robin's position, he writes:

Corey Robin has been spouting nonsense about Trump for 4 years now, showing how little he knows about his own country [alleging] Trump was too incompetent to generate a fascist coup. But he has laid waste to the environment, the rights of working people, and the legal system. More than 70 million people voted for him, and most seem to think he was robbed of a second term. They think the news is fake, all of it. He has by his denial of science, caused at least a quarter million people to die needlessly. He has brought to the surface, with a vengeance, extreme racism, and misogyny. Not to mention his hatred of immigrants, mirrored by his fanatical followers. Robin appears to believe that the left and democracy have never been stronger. He needs to get out of his Brooklyn bubble and its shallow coterie of faux radicals and see the ugly human behavior that is out there and has been encouraged by Trump.[52]

That discourse of denial is an example of the lessons of history being emptied of meaning. This is especially true, says Bill Dixon of the Hannah Arendt Center, since "the all too protean origins of totalitarianism are still with us: loneliness as the normal register of social life, the frenzied lawfulness of ideological certitude, mass poverty and mass homelessness, the routine use of terror as a political instrument, and the ever-growing speeds and scales of media, economics, and warfare."[53] Moreover, the argument ignores the groundwork of forces deployed long before Trump came to power and says little about his massive use of Twitter, the Internet, conservative foundations, and the right-wing media to turn the Republican Party into a group of morally and politically vacuous sycophants. More specifically, it both ignores and underestimates Trumpism's creation of more than 74 million followers who inhabit right-wing populist spaces where "reality can be dispensed and controlled."[54] It also overlooks Trumpism's ability to create cult-like adherents who ignore reason and reality, preferring the image of the strongman who demands unmitigated loyalty and ideological purity.[55]

The power of Trumpism in the cultural realm affirms the success of a new cultural/social formation. It testifies less to the issue of personal incompetence than to Trumpism's success in shaping consciousness among large segments of the American public, and creating regressive modes of identification that strengthen once-marginal elements of a fascist politics and integrate them into centres of governmental power. Thoughtlessness and the collapse of civic culture and moral agency echo a dark period in history in which criminality and corruption entered politics and in which, as Stephen Spender wrote, "the future is like a time bomb buried but ticking away at the present."[56] In the age of Trump, language reinforces the central fascist notion of friend/

enemy distinction as an organizing principle of politics. In this instance, language is used to vilify those considered "other"; the language of environmental justice and racial sensitivity is silenced. More shockingly, Trump used language to imply a moral equivalence between peaceful protesters and the white supremacists and neo-Nazis marching in Charlottesville. At the same time, he employed the language of white supremacists to protest against removing Confederate flags and symbols from the American landscape. There is more at stake here than simply labelling Trump incompetent or ascribing his toxic beliefs and dangerous actions to his narcissistic personality.[57]

Trumpism is a worldview that defines culture as a battleground of losers and winners, a world in which everything is ostensibly rigged against whites.[58] This is a world in which potential unity is obscured in a right-wing assault on the public good, truth, the common good – as reality itself dissolves into a right-wing propaganda machine in which politics becomes "a plot to steal from [whites] their natural due as Americans."[59] Trumpism defines power as immunity from the law; and the most admirable representatives of power are those who are "triumphant and innocent in the face of every accusation of incapacity, criminality and unethical conduct."[60] How else to explain Trump's pardoning of grifters, political cronies, and war criminals?

Far from being the "almost opposite of fascism," Trumpism paves the way for deeply entrenched legacies of hate to be passed on to Trump's followers and future generations. Its goal is to destroy any vestige of democracy as we know it, however flawed, and replace it with a form of neoliberal capital unmoored from any sense of social, political, or ethical standard. What is crucial to recognize is that any starting point for challenging Trumpism and its fascist politics must begin, as Kali Holloway and Martin Mycielski observe, by "recognizing the reality of what is happening … how much damage is being done, how much earth was already scorched … It's good to remember the very big, very frightening picture before us, how far we've already come, and to consider what recourse we have with complicit and corrupt forces standing in the way."[61] As long as Trumpism is endlessly reproduced through the reactionary cultural workstations that generate and distribute its lies, regressive notions of agency, hatred, and disdain for the truth, its afterlife seems assured.

Trumpism represents both a crisis of the civic imagination and an educational crisis. Until it is understood as a cultural crisis rather than being defined as an economic and narrowly political crisis, Trumpism will continue to undermine the ability of individuals and institutions to think critically, question themselves, and produce informed citizens and aligned social movements that can fight collectively for and sustain a radical democracy. There can be no democracy without an educated citizenry, and no democracy can survive under the banner of Trumpism, with its glut of ignorance, commercialization, concentrated power, corporate-owned media, and illusions of freedom.[62]

Gessen, drawing upon history, argues that Trump's electoral defeat offered a choice "between two paths: the path of reckoning and the path of forgetting."[63] The price of forgetting, says Gessen, is too high and would leave in place a rationale for giving immunity to terror, lawlessness, and corruption. To avoid becoming complicit with the crimes of Trumpism, it is necessary to put in place a national project – which would include investigations, hearings, court trials, public assemblies, journalistic inquiries, and other invented formats – to hold accountable those who committed crimes under the Trump regime, including, I would hope, those individuals and politicians who advocated sedition by claiming voter fraud and attempting to overturn the results of the 2020 election.[64] Georgetown University professor Neal Katyal goes further, arguing that Trump should be impeached *again* for trying to illegally overturn the election; the hope would be that he would then be barred from holding any political office in the future.

* * *

Impeaching Trump was a step forward in holding him accountable, but he did not act alone. The broader forces aligned with his ongoing acts of violence, cruelty, and lawlessness must also be held to account: the crimes of Wall Street, the right-wing extremist media conglomerates who lied about the election, and the financial elite who provided the funds for Trump's political and cultural workstations of denial, diversion, and falsehood. The force that Trump deployed to stay in power did not take place in a vacuum. The governing principles of genocide, militarism, and violence have a long history and should also be on trial as a moment of self-reckoning in a time of political and ethical crisis. It is impossible to separate the attack on the Capitol from Trump's language of violence or from the systemic violence characteristic of neoliberal governance in the United States. As intellectual historian Charles H. Clavey observes, violence is a core principle of Trumpism:

At the very heart of Trumpism ... stands the threat of violence: the agitator's constant promise that his followers will visit revenge – in the form of physical harm, political persecution, and social sanction – on those who, they believe, demonized, and excluded them. Violence is both the animating principle of Trumpism and one of Trump's most powerful tools. Trump's most fervent followers, from QAnon conspiracists to white nationalists, glory in the conviction that arrests of prominent Democrats, purges of pedophiles, and pitched street battles against the left are just around the corner. From his assertion that there were "good people on both sides" at Charlottesville to his order that the Proud Boys "stand back and stand by," Trump [showed], time and again, that there is no Trumpism without violence. During an October rally in Michigan, Trump casually remarked that there is "something beautiful" about watching protestors get "pushed around" by the National Guard. "You people get it," he told his loyal followers. "You probably get it better than I do."[65]

It is astonishing that, in the face of Trump's attempt to overthrow the election – which closely resembled the actions of authoritarian regimes around the world – so many academics were resoundingly silent about America being at the tipping point of becoming a full-fledged authoritarian regime. *New York Times* journalist Peter Baker did not miss the threat of authoritarianism posed by Trump's actions in his attempt to overturn an election he decisively lost, even entertaining the use of martial law to do so. Quoting Ruth Ben-Ghiat, author of *Strongmen: From Mussolini to the Present*, Baker writes:

Mr. Trump's efforts ring familiar to many who have studied authoritarian regimes in countries around the world, like those run by President Vladimir V. Putin in Russia and Prime Minister Viktor Orbán in Hungary. "Trump's attempt to overturn the election, and his pressure tactics to that end with Brad Raffensperger, the Georgia secretary of state, are an example of how authoritarianism works in the 21st century ... Today's leaders come in through elections and then manipulate elections to stay in office – until they get enough power to force the hand of legislative bodies to keep them there indefinitely."[66]

With the possibility of instituting various layers of democratic accountability, conditions can be set up not only for a project of truth-telling and answerability but also for a narrative of remembrance in which crimes can be revealed and victims' stories heard. Under such circumstances, the historical record can become an object of critical enquiry, assigning culpability and rectifying moral injury. Such reckoning can also serve as an educational and learning project in which the lessons of the past can create the conditions for connecting education to democratic values, relations, goals, and a redemptive notion of equity and inclusion. Desmond Tutu, in his opening remarks before the convening of South Africa's Truth and Reconciliation Commission in 1996, rightly invoked the power of historical memory and the need to bear witness in the fight against tyranny: "We are charged to unearth the truth about our dark past, to lay the ghosts of the past to rest so that they will not return to haunt us."[67] Education, with its power of reason and its search for truth and justice, is one mechanism for learning from the past and resisting the ghosts ready to re-emerge in the present.

The devaluation of the public good, the continued growth of neo-liberalism's "disimagination machines," the individualizing of social problems, a collective indifference to the rise of the punitive state, the repression of historical consciousness, the failure to engage honestly with the full scope of America's racist history, and the crushing role of racial and economic inequality – all these are fundamentally educational issues. They speak powerfully to the task of changing consciousness by dismantling the depoliticizing forces that render the current social order a world without alternatives. This means, in part, that intellectuals, artists, and other cultural workers must make the work they produce meaningful in order for it to be critical and trans-formative. It demands a revolutionary vision matched by a collective effort to create alternative public spaces that indicate the way common sense works as a taken-for-granted set of normalizing assumptions that prevent people from recognizing the oppressive nature of the societies in which they find themselves. The ideological tyranny and the cultural politics of Trumpism demand a wholesale revision of how education and democracy mutually inform each other. They need to be understood as part of a broader politics that can create a world in which the oppressed are heard and the voices of those who suffer find a public space for articulation.

Any movement for resistance needs to become more accessible to working-class people, and there is a crucial need to connect personal and political rights with economic rights. Only as a social state that guarantees rights for everyone can democracy survive. The question of who holds power, and how power is separated from politics – with politics being local and power being global – has to be addressed as a condition for international resistance. Neoliberal capitalism has morphed into a form of Trumpism which produces zones of abandonment where individuals become unknowable and faceless, and lack human rights.

Under Trumpism, society increasingly reproduces pedagogical "death zones of humanity" that triumph not only in violence but also ignorance and irrationality.[68] These are zones that undermine people's capacity to speak, write, and act from a position of empowerment and be responsible to themselves and others. To counter this form of depoliticization, there is a need for modes of civic education and critical literacy that provide the bridging work between thinking critically and the possibility of interpretation as intervention. Critical pedagogy is a moral and political practice committed to the realization that there is no resistance without hope, and no hope without a vision of an alternative society rooted in the ideals of justice, equality, and freedom.

Trumpism evokes the shadow of authoritarianism in the form of a resurgent fascist politics that dehumanizes all of us in the face of a refusal to confront its spectre of racism, lawlessness, and brutality. Trump's impeachments were only the beginning of confronting the fascist ghosts of the past which Trump proved are no longer in the shadows or on the margins of American politics. The evident truth that the influence and legacy of Trumpism will long outlast the aftermath of Trump's presidency makes it all the more urgent to reclaim the redemptive elements of government responsibility, democratic ideals, and the public spheres that make a radical democracy possible.

In the current historical moment, the time has come to reclaim the great utopian ideals unleashed by a long history of civil rights struggles, the insights and radical struggles produced by the Black Lives Matter movement. There is a need to rethink and relearn the trajectory of history by considering the role that critical education and notions of civic literacy have played in producing a collective anti-capitalist consciousness. At stake is the crucial project of once again creating the critical agents and social movements that refuse to equate capitalism and democracy and which uphold the conviction that ecological destruction, mass poverty, militarism, systemic racism, and a host of other social problems cannot be solved by leaving capitalism in place. Only then can mass movements arise in which the future can be written in the language of justice, compassion, and the fundamental narratives of freedom and equality.

NOTES

1 Mike Ludwig, "The Trumps Have Fueled a Far-Right Media Monster That Is Not Going Away," *Truthout*, 6 January 2021, https://truthout.org/articles/the-trumps-have-fueled-a-far-right-media-monster-that-is-not-going-away/.

2 Will Steakin, "Trump Allies Helped Plan, Promote Rally That Led to Capitol Attack," ABC *News*, 10 January 2021, https://readersupportednews.org/news-section2/318-66/67209-focus-trump-allies-helped-plan-promote-rally-that-led-to-capitol-attack.

3 Ed Pilkington, "Incitement: A Timeline of Trump's Inflammatory Rhetoric Before the Capitol Riot," *The Guardian*, 7 January 2021, https://www.theguardian.com/us-news/2021/jan/07/trump-incitement-inflammatory-rhetoric-capitol-riot.

4 Ed Pilkington, "'Stand Back and Stand By': How Trumpism Led to the Capitol Siege," *The Guardian*, 6 January 2021, https://www.theguardian.com/us-news/2021/jan/06/donald-trump-armed-protest-capitol.

5 Karissa Bell, "Twitter Suspends Donald Trump," *Yahoo.Com*, 6 January 2021, https://www.nytimes.com/2021/01/06/opinion/trump-capitol-dc-protests.html.

6 Editorial Board, "Trump Is to Blame for the Capitol Attack," *New York Times*, 6 January 2021, https://www.nytimes.com/2021/01/06/opinion/trump-capitol-dc-protests.html.

7 Timothy Snyder, "The American Abyss," *New York Times*, 9 January 2021, https://www.nytimes.com/2021/01/09/magazine/trump-coup.html.

8 Samuel Farber, "Trumpism Will Endure," *Jacobin*, 3 January 2021, https://jacobinmag.com/2021/01/donald-trump-white-working-class-trumpism.

9 Ibid.

10 Kenny Stancil, "Poll Shows Nearly Half of GOP Voters – Lied to by Right-Wing Media – Approve of US Capitol Ransacking," *Common Dreams*, 7 January 2021, https://www.commondreams.org/news/2021/01/07/poll-shows-nearly-half-gop-voters-lied-right-wing-media-approve-us-capitol.

11 Charlie Warzel, "The Pro-Trump Movement Was Always Headed Here," *New York Times*, 6 January 2021, https://www.nytimes.com/2021/01/06/opinion/protests-trump-disinformation.html.

12 David Theo Goldberg, "On Civil War," *Talking Violence Podcast*, 5 January 2021, https://talkingviolence.podbean.com/e/ep-7-on-civil-war-david-theo-goldberg/.

13 Anthony DiMaggio, "The Coup in Washington: Why Is Anyone Surprised by Trump's Fascist Politics?" *CounterPunch*, 7 January 2021, https://www.counterpunch.org/2021/01/07/the-coup-in-washington-why-is-anyone-surprised-by-trumps-fascist-politics/.

14 Masha Gessen, "Why America Needs a Reckoning with the Trump Era," *The New Yorker*, 10 November 2020, https://www.newyorker.com/news/our-columnists/why-america-needs-a-reckoning-with-the-trump-era.

15 Becky Z. Dernbach and Jeremy Schulman, "The Shockingly Long List of Corrupt Officials and Political Allies Pardoned by Trump," *Mother Jones*, 22 December 2020, https://www.motherjones.com/politics/2020/12/trump-pardons-hunter-collins-stockman-blackwater/.

16 Jennifer Evans, "Trump Lost, but Racism Is Alive and Infused in U.S. History," *The Conversation*, 10 November 2020, https://theconversation.com/trump-lost-but-racism-is-alive-and-infused-in-u-s-history-149249.

17 Sophia Ankel, "Trump Promises 'Wild' Protests in Washington, DC, on the Day Congress Is Set to Finalize Election Results," *Yahoo! News*, 20 December 2020, https://news.yahoo.com/trump-promises-wild-protests-washington-165055313.html.

18 Noam Chomsky, "On Trump's Disastrous Coronavirus Response, WHO, China, Gaza and Global Capitalism," *Democracy Now*, 25 May 2020, https://www.democracynow.org/2020/5/25/noam_chomsky_on_trump_s_disastrous.

19 Teo Armus, "Unaccompanied Migrant Children Suffer 'Inhumane and Cruel Experience' in CBP Custody, Report Alleges," *Washington Post*, 30 October 2020, https://www.washingtonpost.com/nation/2020/10/30/migrant-children-border-unaccompanied/.

20 Masha Gessen, *Surviving Autocracy* (New York: Riverhead Books, 2020), 58.

21 William I. Robinson, *The Global Police State* (London: Pluto Press, 2020), 123.

22 Ashton Carter, Dick Cheney, William Cohen, Mark Esper, Robert Gates, Chuck Hagel, James Mattis, Leon Panetta, William Perry, and Donald Rumsfeld, "All 10 Living Former Defense Secretaries: Involving the Military in Election Disputes Would Cross into Dangerous Territory,"

Washington Post, 3 January 2021, https://www.washingtonpost.com/
opinions/10-former-defense-secretaries-military-peaceful-transfer-of-
power/2021/01/03/2a23d52e-4c4d-11eb-a9f4-0e668b9772ba_
story.html. See also, Jennifer Rubin, "It's Impeachable. It's Likely
Illegal. It's a Coup," *Washington Post*, 3 January 2021, https://www.
washingtonpost.com/opinions/2021/01/03/its-impeachable-its-likely-
illegal-its-coup/.

23 Edward-Isaac Dovere, "How Joe Biden Watched the Capitol Assault,"
    The Atlantic, 6 January 2021, https://www.thcatlantic.com/politics/
    archive/2021/01/joe-biden-responded-storming-capitol/617575/.

24 Tim Nichols, "Worse Than Treason," *The Atlantic*, 4 January 2021,
    https://www.theatlantic.com/ideas/archive/2021/01/what-republicans-
    are-doing-worse-treason/617538/.

25 Federico Finchelstein, *A Brief History of Fascist Lies* (Oakland: University
    of California Press, 2020).

26 Gessen, *Surviving Autocracy*, 17–18.

27 Ishaan Tharoor with Ruby Mellen, "Trump Joins Dictators and
    Demagogues in Touting 'Patriotic Education,'" *Washington Post*,
    21 September 2020, accessed 15 July 2021, https://www.washingtonpost.
    com/world/2020/09/21/trump-patriotic-education-china-orban/; Aamer
    Madhani and Deb Riechmann, "Trump Pushes 'Patriotic Education'
    While Downplaying History of U.S. Slavery," *Global News*, 17 September
    2020, https://globalnews.ca/news/7342896/trump-patriotic-education-
    slavery/.

28 Ishaan Tharoor with Ruby Mell, "Trump Joins Dictators and
    Demagogues in Touting 'Patriotic Education,'" *Washington Post*,
    21 September 2020, https://www.washingtonpost.com/world/2020/09/21/
    trump-patriotic-education-china-orban/.

29 The Editorial Board, "The Wreckage Betsy DeVos Leaves Behind," *New
    York Times*, 2 January 2021, https://www.nytimes.com/2021/01/02/
    opinion/sunday/education-department-cardona-biden.html.

30 Jane Mayer, "The Making of the Fox News White House," *The New
    Yorker*, 4 March 2019, https://www.newyorker.com/magazine/2019/03/11/
    the-making-of-the-fox-news-white-house; Michael I. Niman, "Weaponized
    Social Media Is Driving the Explosion of Fascism," *Truthout*, 5 April 2019,
    https://truthout.org/articles/weaponized-social-media-is-driving-the-explosion-
    of-fascism/.

31 Amelia Mertha, "Watch This Space: Spectacle and Speed on the Internet,"
    Honi Soit, 18 October 2020, https://honisoit.com/2020/10/watch-this-
    space-spectacle-and-speed-on-the-internet/.

32 Matt Taibbi, *Hate Inc.: Why Today's Media Makes Us Despise One Another* (New York: OR Books, 2019).

33 Guy Debord, *Society of the Spectacle* (New York: Black & Red, 2002).

34 One particularly egregious reading of this sort can be found in the work of Ross Douthat, "Donald Trump Doesn't Want Authority," *New York Times*, May 2019, https://www.nytimes.com/2020/05/19/opinion/coronavirus-trump-orban.html.

35 Norman Solomon, "In 2021, the Best Way to Fight Neofascist Republicans Is to Fight Neoliberal Democrats," *Reader Supported News*, 4 January 2021, https://readersupportednews.org/opinion2/277-75/67103-rsn-in-2021-the-best-way-to-fight-neofascist-republicans-is-to-fight-neoliberal-democrats.

36 Samuel Moyn, "How Trump Won," *New York Review of Books*, 9 November 2020, https://www.nybooks.com/daily/2020/11/09/how-trump-won/.

37 Saharra Griffin and Malkie Wall, "President's Trump's Anti-Worker Agenda," *Center for American Progress Action Fund*, 19 August 2019, https://www.americanprogressaction.org/issues/economy/reports/2019/08/28/174893/president-trumps-anti-worker-agenda/.

38 A brilliant analysis of this issue can be found in John Bellamy Foster, *Trump in the White House: Tragedy and Farce* (New York: Monthly Review Press, 2018).

39 Moyn, "How Trump Won"; Jeet Heer, "Even as a Weak President, Trump Has Undermined Democracy," *The Nation*, 28 December 2020, https://www.thenation.com/article/politics/trump-weak-undermine-democracy/.

40 See especially Sarah Churchwell, "American Fascism: It Has Happened Again," *New York Review of Books*, 26 May 2020, https://www.nybooks.com/daily/2020/06/22/american-fascism-it-has-happened-here/. See also Paul Street, "We Have a Fascism Problem," *CounterPunch*, 16 December 2020, https://www.counterpunch.org/2020/12/16/we-have-a-fascism-problem/; Timothy Snyder, *On Tyranny: Twenty Lessons from the Twentieth Century* (New York: Tim Duggan Books, 2017); Jason Stanley, *How Fascism Works* (New York: Random House, 2018); and Henry A. Giroux, *American Nightmare: Facing the Challenge of Fascism* (Chicago: City Lights Books, 2018).

41 Richard J. Evans, "Why Trump Isn't a Fascist," *New Statesman*, 13 January 2021, https://www.newstatesman.com/world/2021/01/why-trump-isnt-fascist.

42 Timothy Snyder, "The American Abyss," *New York Times*, 9 January 2021, https://www.nytimes.com/2021/01/09/magazine/trump-coup.html.

43 Cited in Terry Eagleton, "Reappraisals: What Is the Worth of Social Democracy?" *Harper's Magazine*, October 2010, 78.

44 Robert Jay Lifton, *Losing Reality: On Cults, Cultism, and the Mindset of Political and Religious Zealotry* (New York: New Press, 2019), 1.

45 Ibid.

46 Frank Bruni, "We Still Don't Really Understand Trump – or America," *New York Times*, 7 November 2020, https://www.nytimes.com/2020/11/07/opinion/sunday/trump-election-performance.html.

47 Coco Das, "What Are You Going to Do about the Nazi Problem?" *Refuse Fascism*, 24 November 2020, https://refusefascism.org/2020/11/24/what-are-you-going-to-do-about-the-nazi-problem/.

48 David Klion, "Almost the Opposite of Fascism," *Jewish Currents*, 26 November 2020, https://jewishcurrents.org/almost-the-complete-opposite-of-fascism/.

49 Ibid.

50 Richard A. Etlin, "Introduction: The Perverse Logic of Nazi Thought," in *Art, Culture, and Media under the Third Reich*, ed. Richard A. Etlin (Chicago: University of Chicago Press, 2002), 8.

51 Fintan O'Toole, "Trial Runs for Fascism Are in Full Flow," *Irish Times*, 26 June 2018, https://www.irishtimes.com/opinion/fintan-o-toole-trial-runs-for-fascism-are-in-full-flow-1.3543375.

52 Michael Yates, personal correspondence, 15 December 2020.

53 Bill Dixon, "Totalitarianism and the Sandstorm," *Hannah Arendt Center*, 3 February 2014, http://www.hannaharendtcenter.org/?p=12466.

54 Lifton, *Losing Reality: On Cults, Cultism, and the Mindset of Political and Religious Zealotry*, 1.

55 Ruth Ben-Ghiat, "Fascism Scholar: Strongman Trump Radicalized His Supporters; Turning This Back Will Be Very Hard," *Democracy Now*, 11 January 2021, https://www.democracynow.org/2021/1/11/trump_impeachment_pelosi_pence.

56 Cited in Elisabeth Young-Bruehl, *Why Arendt Matters* (New York: Integrated Publishing Solutions, 2006), 149.

57 Ken Wolf, "Evaluating Trump's Personal Legacy," *Mercury Ledger & Times*, 2 November 2020, https://www.murrayledger.com/opinion/evaluating-trump-s-personal-legacy/article_2e1c8682-1d39-11eb-ab7e-23ab9a51d4de.html.

58 Fintan O'Toole, "Democracy's Afterlife," *New York Review of Books*, 3 December 2020, https://www.nybooks.com/articles/2020/12/03/democracys-afterlife/.

59 Chauncey DeVega, "Irish Author Fintan O'Toole Explains the 'Suspension of Disbelief' That Made Trump's Destruction of America Possible," *Alternet*, 26 May 2020, https://www.alternet.org/2020/05/irish-author-fintan-otoole-explains-the-suspension-of-disbelief-that-made-trumps-destruction-of-america-possible.

60 Judith Butler, "Genius or Suicide," *London Review of Books* 41, no. 20 (October 2019), https://www.lrb.co.uk/the-paper/v41/n20/judith-butler/genius-or-suicide.

61 Kali Holloway and Martin Mycielski, "Increasingly a Necessity: A 15-Point Guide to Surviving Authoritarianism," *Moyers on Democracy*, 15 December 2017, https://billmoyers.com/story/increasingly-necessity-15-point-guide-surviving-authoritarianism/.

62 Wendy Brown, *Undoing the Demos: Neoliberalism's Stealth Revolution* (New York: Zone Books, 2015), 178–9.

63 Gessen, "Why America Needs a Reckoning with the Trump Era."

64 For different views on such accountability, see Jill Lepore, "Let History, Not Partisans, Prosecute Trump," *The New Yorker*, 16 October 2020, https://www.washingtonpost.com/outlook/truth-reconciliation-tribunal-trump-historians/2020/10/16/84026810-0e88-11eb-b1e8-16b59b92b36d_story.html; and Elie Mystal, "We're Going to Need a Truth and Reconciliation Commission to Recover from Trump," *The Nation*, 20 October 2020, https://www.thenation.com/article/politics/trump-truth-reconciliation/.

65 Charles H. Clavey, "Donald Trump, Our Prophet of Deceit," *Boston Review*, 20 October 2020, https://www.bostonreview.net/articles/charles-h-clavey-what-frankfurt-school-would-say-about-trump/.

66 Peter Baker, "An Insurgency from Inside the Oval Office." *New York Times*, 4 January 2020, https://www.nytimes.com/2021/01/04/us/politics/trump-white-house.html.

67 Cited in L. Robert Block Johannesburg, "South Africa Begins Laying Ghosts to Rest," *Independent*, 25 April 1996, https://www.independent.co.uk/news/world/south-africa-begins-laying-ghosts-to-rest-1305130.html.

68 Etienne Balibar, "Outline of a Topography of Cruelty: Citizenship and Civility in the Era of Global Violence," in *We, the People of Europe? Reflections on Transnational Citizenship*, trans. James Swenson (Princeton: Princeton University Press, 2004), 115–32.

2

The Ebb of the Old Liberal Order and the Horizon of New Possibilities for Freedom

Katerina Kolozova

It is not an easy task to explain to my North American friends that there is an ideological project that terms itself "illiberalism," championed by Hungarian prime minister Viktor Orbán and other notorious European autocrats such Matteo Salvini, Marine le Pen, and Jarosław Kaczyński, which stands *for the opposite of what the declaredly left anti-liberalism advocates*. It is conservative; it opposes migration, racial and cultural diversity, gender equality and diversity; it is populist, embracing strong and authoritarian leaders. This type of illiberalism, which is not typical of Eastern and Central Europe alone but has also taken hold in the west of the continent too,[1] dismisses values such as freedom of the press, freedom of expression, and academic autonomy as values a true democracy can and should do without. The illiberals uphold democracy as a political form devoid of liberal values. The "illiberal democracy"[2] repositions liberalism in the past, and by doing so it also frequently uses a language indistinguishable from that of the left critique of "global neoliberalism." European leaders of this stripe were staunch supporters of Donald Trump. One of their intellectual figureheads is the French philosopher and journalist, often identified as fascist, Alain de Benoist, who, in his latest book, *Contre le libéralisme*,[3] mobilizes Marx next to the likes of Julius Evola and Alexandr Dugin in virtue of a takedown of global (neo)liberalism.

It is never an easy task to paint this entire picture, in its rich complexity, to my left-wing North American friends and colleagues because they too have long despised "liberalism," a supposed *ethos* rather than a political doctrine itself. Certainly, liberal political theories have been subject to their critique as well; however, in such discussions too, I have noticed, the target is essentially the presumed *ethos* rather than the argument of liberalism. The *ethos* is habitually identified in rhetorical tropes that betray a bourgeois reason – spontaneously equated with liberal – whereas the "academic discussion" comes down to some references to the famous critiques from the 1990s of Kant's autonomous reason and also to economic reductionism. I am speaking of personal exchanges here and cannot quote, but I mention them to illustrate conversations that might be familiar to the reader as well.

Certainly, these North American friends of mine do not see their illiberalism as anything of the sort described at the beginning of the present paper – so they start searching for different denominations for a political project that has defined its purpose and named itself "illiberal." Those who would want to successfully oppose the autocrats have therefore found themselves bereft of a language to do so, since defending freedom of expression, freedom of the press, and individual freedoms suppressed by authoritarian rule sounds like a very liberal thing to do. Matters become more complicated when one takes into consideration the fact that the far right have made appeals to freedom of expression too – even though, paradoxically, only to attack liberalism, and, by so doing, attacking the left for being guilty of liberalism.

I was born and grew up in the Socialist Federative Republic of Yugoslavia, and as a high school student in the mid-1980s I became habituated to identifying liberation or true human liberty with the true communism my former country failed to realize, even by the admission of the Communist Party of Yugoslavia itself. As soon as the former Eastern Bloc in Europe, including the non-aligned Yugoslavia, was "liberated" from communism, our own Marxist voices, including those critical of the ruling doctrine, and the practice too, simply vanished. Admittedly, we were ashamed of Marxism's failure. In perfect coincidence with this rising shame, we were also immediately exposed to a proper Europeanization – through the EU accession processes – and thus we embraced Western academia too, and ever so eagerly.

We, the failed communist societies, admitted our moral defeat and conceded to the call-out of the post-Marxists such as Alasdair MacIntyre: "Marxism had failed morally," apparently more so than the West. MacIntyre's critical project seems to rely on all but Marxism:

Aristotle, Nietzsche, and very little – if any – Marx or Marxism, whereas his main charge against it is that it has remained "too liberal." Therefore, when it comes to the admission of Marxism's failure, there is an overlooked misunderstanding between us in the East and the "post"-Marxists of the West. Whereas we in the East believed for so long that we had failed because of the "bureaucratized and alienated state" and its suppression of the freedom of expression – its totalitarianism, put simply – MacIntyre and his acolytes accuse our former political system/s of the opposite, of being too liberal.

Let us note that MacIntyre's premise is not entirely derived from the assumption that the mode of production had not moved away substantially from the liberal model (through wage labour and commodity production, for example). His reprimand is that the underlying reason for Marxism's failure is that the *ethos* of the former communist states, its morality, has "remained too liberal."[4] Apparently, it is insufficient totalitarianism that has led communism to its "moral failure" (rather than a historic failure related to the mode of production). Sadly, the Anglo-American interpretation of Marxism's failure, declared almost simultaneously with Fukuyama's declaration of the end of history, has become the paradigm of the global "radical left" critique of liberalism – based on very little Marx and lots of Aristotle, as well as very little political economy and lots of ethics and morality.[5]

Then again, Marx and Engels emphasized repeatedly that communism was not about any form of morality, but rather about the social organization, cultural transformation, and perhaps moral revalorization that would ensue from an economy that would not be based on wage labour, as Takahisa Oishi demonstrates in his meticulous exegesis of Marx's original text, reconstructing a unity of a rather fragmented argument.[6] The following statement could not be more unequivocal:

> The communists do not preach *morality* at all, as Stirner does so extensively. They do not put to people the moral demand: love one another, do not be egoists, etc.; on the contrary, they are very well aware that egoism, just as much as selflessness, is in definite circumstances a necessary form of the self-assertion of individuals. Hence, the communists by no means want, as Saint Max believes ... to do away with the "private individual" for the sake of the "general," selfless man.[7]

Oishi's reading of Marx on the subject of morality being one of the materializations – in the form of social relations – of the different modes of production leads to the conclusion that it is the socialist economic foundation composed of "associations of individual workers"[8] that provides the basis for a possible new ethics. This thesis is further explored by Igor Shoikhedbrod in his 2019 publication which proffers an important addition and further corroboration to Oishi's main thesis.[9] It is important to note that Oishi undertakes the painstaking task of distinguishing Marx's enunciations and arguments from those present in Engel's interpretations and offers the following formulaic summarization:

> The French version begins with "the capitalist mode of production and of appropriation that corresponds to it is ..." and omits the "free workers." The present German and the English versions were rewritten or modified by Engels. As far as we can distinguish a mode of appropriation from its basis and understand it in its context, we cannot agree with Dühring more: "individual private property (as founded on the labour of its proprietor)" is negated by "capitalist private property (which rests on the exploitation of alien, but formally free labour)," and then by "individual property (on the basis of ... cooperation and the free workers" possession in common of the land and the means of production produced by labour itself)" = "social property."
> Let us formulate this and compare it with that of Engels:
>
> Marx: *individual property = social property ≠ common property*
> Engels: *individual property ≠ social property = common property.*[10]

Oishi's philological and philosophical reconstruction of Marx's argument seems to me, as someone who was born and reached adulthood in Yugoslavia, more in tune with what I remember my former country set as its horizon and where our collective post-communist self feels, at least predominantly, to have failed. In other words, more liberty would have been considered as bringing us closer to the communist ideal through the form of self-management characteristic of the latest stage of Yugoslavia's economic development. Such spontaneous interpretation or reminiscence on my part would be in line with Paulin Clochec's brilliant analysis of "Marx's liberalism," which manages to demonstrate that what Marx sought to accomplish through his critique of (bourgeois) liberalism was full radicalization of the most basic tenet of the liberal ideal, that of liberty embodied by individuals and collectives in an inextricable manner.[11]

The very possibility of criticizing "liberalism" and "liberal values" while having different and even opposing referents in mind speaks to the fact that the notion is multifaceted and embedded in different political doctrines. For example, Viktor Orbán's attack on academic liberties because they are "unpatriotic," "sponsored by George Soros," and "seeking to undermine European civilization" is incomparable with the Western progressive left's critique of liberalism, which seeks to radicalize individual gendered and multicultural self-expression. Returning to Marxism, let us note that what Marx and his disciples have been tackling all along is the possibility of imagining freedom, liberties, and arguably rights (as well as *das Recht* as in rule of law) in communism as well as engaging in a critique of bourgeois liberalism. It seems as if Marxist scholarship has been able to conceive of some generic notions of freedom, liberty, and a sublated (*aufgehoben*) version of liberalism, emerging from the contradictions of capitalism and bourgeois society in a dialectical and historically determined manner. If such a generalization is inapplicable to the entire legacy – or to all of the legacies – of Marxism, it certainly is, I would argue, applicable to Marx's own writings. I am basing this argument not only on the convincing exegeses of authors such as Oishi and Clochec, but also on Marx's oeuvre itself, in particular *On the Jewish Question*, *The Holy Family* (co-written with Engels), and *Grundrisse*, among others.

We are thus brought to the matter at hand and its context at the turn of the third decade of the twenty-first century: in an era of rising "illiberalisms" (of different sorts, as I tried to illustrate here in my opening paragraphs), and possible further suspension of rights due to the prolonged COVID pandemic and/or the recovery from it, are we not faced with the challenge of defending some very generic freedoms such as the freedom to move? How are we to do so beyond the already irreparable language of liberalism? Can we speak a new language of freedom and of specific yet rather generic liberties? And is it possible to do so by way of discarding the entire history of liberalism and its fundamental concepts?

To be clear, I am not advocating unreasonable defiance of pandemic containment control. I am not saying that we should put our right to freely displace our bodies and enjoy social and physical interaction above the collective health – my warning is that the pandemic may be abused in order to limit some of said basic and apparently generic forms of freedom. In fact, warnings of abuse of the pandemic for a democratic backsliding and imposition of authoritarian rule were sounded as early as the spring of 2020.[12] We could say, therefore, that there is a twofold pressing reason to invent a language of freedom that will transcend the confines of liberal traditions, both their affirmations and their critiques as aspects of the same historical given. Furthermore, Marx's radicalization of the "liberal core" found in the discussions of the Young Hegelians, when taken beyond the bourgeois status quo and its material-economic foundation, provides the means for it, as demonstrated by Clochec.[13]

In order for such a radicalization of the concept to take place, one ought to create the conditions for the first prerequisite – the transformation of the mode of production, whereby the means of production would be seized by *associations of individual producers*. If, at the present point in time, such a possibility seems utopian, let us recall that Marx himself argued that associations of free producers could appear within the capitalist model. Namely, in the first volume of *Capital*, Marx states that "individual private property" is "the foundation of small-scale industry, and small-scale industry is a necessary condition for the development of social production and of the free individuality of the worker himself."[14] The expansion of the small-scale industry of associations of free workers would deepen the capitalist contradiction and ultimately lead to its resolution and to a transformation of the political-economic paradigm. Such very material freedom is premised on mere physical freedom of movement and the establishment of social relations. In order to achieve such freedom in our emerging post-COVID world dominated by a variety of illiberalisms, we must re-establish Marx's critique of the division between the dbourgeois state and civil society, which amounts to the state's alienation from its citizens (who are relegated to the apolitical or post-political civil society).[15] The split at issue – and the problem of the alienated and alienating state – can be overcome by the social relations ensuing from the free producers' associations developing into more than a mere technology of "administering things" (Engels)[16] that submits to society as a self-management system of all socio-economic relations rather than the modern State.[17]

It is a historical struggle, but I see no reason to view historical transformations and progressions as necessarily linear. Therefore, reclaiming a language of liberty in the face of rising authoritarianisms and the transformation of the mode of production could take place by following the laws of both "synchrony and diachrony,"[18] as Claude Levi-Strauss put it. If the present paradigm is in crisis and the germs of new possibilities emerge from its very entropy, islands of potential exist on the economic plane as well as the plane of social relations, both of them seen as unequivocally material.

NOTES

1 Consider the success of the new left parties, the populists, sovereigntist euro-skeptic parties in the 2019 European parliamentary elections.
2 Not in the sense used by Fareed Zakaria in his 1997 piece for *Foreign Affairs*, but rather in the sense given to it by Viktor Orbán in his speech at the 29th Bálványos Summer Open University and Student Camp, Website of the Hungarian Government (29 July 2018), available at https://www.kormany.hu/en/the-prime-minister/the-prime-minister-s-speeches/prime-minister-viktor-orban-s-speech-at-the-29th-balvanyos-summer-open-university-and-student-camp, accessed on 11 April 2020.
3 Alain de Benoist, *Contre le libéralisme* (Monaco: Le Rocher, 2019).
4 Alasdair MacIntyre, *After Virtue: A Study in Moral Theory* (Notre Dame, IN: University of Notre Dame Press, 1984; London: Duckworth, 1985), 2nd edition, ix–x.
5 Kelvin Knight, "The Ethical Post-Marxism of Alasdair MacIntyre," in *Marxism, the Millennium and Beyond*, ed. Mark Cowling and Paul Reynolds (Basingstoke and New York: Palgrave Publishers, 2000), 74–96.
6 Takahisa Oishi, *The Unknown Marx: Reconstructing a Unified Perspective* (London: Pluto Press in Association with Takushoku Univeristy in Tokyo, 2000), 154–64.
7 Karl Marx and Frederick Engels, *German Ideology in Collected Works,* trans. Richard Dixon et al., 50 vols. (New York: International Publishers, 1979–2004), 5–24.
8 Karl Marx, "Capital and Labor," in *Karl Marx and Friedrich Engels Gesamtausgabe* (Berlin: Dietz, 1972). Thus individual property is re-established, but on the basis of the achievements of the modern mode of production. So we have an association of free workers who possess in common the land and the means of production produced by labour itself. Oishi's translation; quotation is borrowed from Takahisa Oishi, *The Unknown Marx*, 157.

9 Igor Shoikhedbrod, *Revisiting Marx's Critique of Liberalism: Rethinking Justice, Legality and Rights* (London: Palgrave Macmillan, 2019).

10 Oishi, *The Unknown Marx,* 156. (My emphasis in italic, in order to distinguish visually the formulaic statements, following the visual emphasis in the original, accomplished through line spacing.)

11 Paulin Clochec, "Le libéralisme de Marx," *Actuel Marx* 2, no. 56 (2014): 109–23.

12 Amanda B. Edgell, Anna Lührmann, and Seraphine F. Maerz, "Policy Brief No. #23: Pandemic Backsliding: Does Covid-19 Put Democracy at Risk?," *V-Dem Institute/Variety of Democracy Institute, Department of Political Science*, Gothenburg, Sweden, 2020, https://www.v-dem.net/media/filer_public/52/eb/52eb913a-b1ad-4e55-9b4b-3710ff70d1bf/pb_23.pdf; Florian Bieber et al., "Policy Brief: The Western Balkans in Times of the Global Pandemic," *Balkans in Europe Policy Advisory Group*, April 2020, https://biepag.eu/wp-content/uploads/2020/04/BiEPAG-Policy-Brief-The-Western-Balkans-in-Times-of-the-Global-Pandemic.pdf.

13 Clochec, "Le libéralisme de Marx," 118–23.

14 Karl Marx (1976), *Capital*, Vol. 1, trans. Ben Fowkes (London: Penguin Group, 1976), 927.

15 Clochec, "Le libéralisme de Marx," 115.

16 Frederick Engels, "Socialism: Utopian and Scientific," in *Collected Works*, ed. Karl Marx and Frederick Engels, trans. Richard Dixon et al., 50 vols. (New York: International Publishers, 1979–2004), 24–321.

17 Marx, *Capital*, 927.

18 Claude Levi-Strauss, *The Savage Mind* (Letchworth: Weidenfeld and Nicolson Ltd, 1966), 63–71.

3

Constitutionalism:
Jurisgenesis as Polisgenesis

Eduardo Mendieta

For every constitution there is an epic, for each decalogue a scripture. Once understood in the context of the narratives that give it meaning, law becomes not merely a system of rules to be observed, but a world in which we live. In this normative world, law and narrative are inseparably related.

Robert Cover[1]

The storming and sacking of the US Capitol on 6 January 2021 was no storming of the Bastille. There were no prisoners there, only elected officials preparing to certify an election that all credible press, election officials, judges, and so forth had confirmed and certified was the most fair and legal election in American history. January 6 was no revolutionary action, but a counter-revolution, and above all, an anti-democratic and anti-constitutional insurrection. The iconography and visuals of the insurrectionists leave little doubt as to why the crowd was rioting at the Capitol. Outside they had built a hanging platform; they had come to enact the "people's justice." Since then, we have slowly learned about the level of coordination between the then Trump White House and the MAGA insurrectionists. January 6 was not a demonstration but a deliberate attempt at a *coup d'état* that nearly succeeded.[2]

As events unfolded that day, some journalists and politicians claimed that what occurred at the Capitol was the work of Antifa, and that a double standard was being used vis-à-vis Black Lives Matter. Most people don't know what Antifa is, or whether it exists, or is a movement, and whether they are armed or trained to overthrow the government. We do know, in contrast, that many of the people who stormed the Capitol are part of white-supremacist groups that are armed and ready to engage in civil war. But, most significantly, the question has been raised: can we compare the B L M protests that erupted after decades of police violence against African Americans and Brown folk with the violence of alleged protesters at the January 6 insurrection? Are these movements comparable? Can we really think of them as analogous forms of "speaking out"? What is the platform from which we – any one of us – speak out, and how is that platform built and for whom, and to proclaim what with what means? These are the meta-questions presented to us by all insurrections against all constitutions.

The constitutions that were written in the aftermath of the American, French, and Haitian revolutions may have been responses to historically contingent events, but ever since their enactment they have unleashed normative forces that remain in effect, still unexhausted. Those revolutions spread the mantle of the rule of law over peoples, which then became nation-states and slowly turned into constitutional states. It is because of them that, as Robert Cover put it, we inhabit "a *nomos*, a normative universe."[3] The violence, terror, and genocides of the twentieth century have confirmed the fragility of constitutions, but they have also demonstrated their unsurpassed ability to domesticate political power and pacify through juridification interactions among peoples, nations, and states. Arguably, since the Second World War we have lived in an age of state constitutionalism and the slow but steady rise of cosmopolitan constitutionalism under the guidance of the new global regimen of human rights.[4] Constitutions address one of the most fundamental problems of politics – and here we would do well to quote one of the best and still indispensable constitutional theorists, Alexander Hamilton: the problem of "whether societies of men are really capable or not, of establishing good government from reflection and choice, or whether they are forever destined to depend, for their political constitutions, on accident and force."[5] Constitutions affirm that governments are and ought to be the result of deliberation and choice, and not of accident and force.

In what follows, I want first to briefly discuss some general characteristics of constitutions and constitutionalism by highlighting key elements of the US Constitution; then, in a second step, I want to focus on what I will call the de-fetishizing and de-mystifying force of constitutions. Constitutions unmask at least five fetishes of modern societies. In so doing they carry out the secularization of all state coercion, transforming power into authority. Constitutions proclaim that all political power is the power of a community that binds itself to the rule of law. They enable "self-rule" (political autonomy), through "law-rule" (the rule of law), to use legal scholar Frank Michelman's felicitous expression.[6] At the same time that constitutions are jurisgenerative they are also temporal devices that bind generations across time. In this way they are what I will call polisgenerative. Constitutionalism is as much about making law as it is about constituting the political, the sphere within which peoples can forge a common future.

JURISGENESIS AS POLISGENESIS

Constitutionalism is the name given to "a set of theories, values, principles, and institutions that are concerned with the authorization, organization, direction, and constraint of political power."[7] It also names the tradition of "constituting" political units. In this sense, constitutionalism has a long pre-history, namely the history of generating, authorizing, and binding political authority.[8] But before there was constitutionalism, there were constitutions, those written in the eighteenth century in particular: the French, the American, and the Haitian. It is for this reason that we should distinguish between two senses of the term "constitutionalism." One sense refers to empirical, or historically given political conditions; for instance, the separation of powers or their absence. This sense is descriptive. The other sense refers to the making of laws that establish and authorize political authority; setting it up, for instance, that all law-making is subject to constitutional review. This sense is normative.[9] Constitutions, interestingly, are written documents, but they are also aspirational proclamations; namely, mandating that the constituted government will be under the "rule of law." Thus, the empirical and normative dimensions are intermingled – which is why, where there is a constitution, there is constitutionalism.

Constitutional systems have the following essential and indispensable elements: i) institutions that are granted powers that are accountable to the people; ii) horizontal disaggregation of government powers that sets the norm of a government that is self-limiting; that is, legislative, executive, and judicial branches of government, with their respective powers, limits, duties, and responsibilities; iii) the submission of all delegated powers to the rule of law under the watch-ful eye of the constitution itself. Constitutional systems may also include some of the following elements, some of which follow from the prior basic three elements; iv) non-statist conception of sover-eignty, for all authority derives from the people; v) the imperative of judicial review which overviews the legality of the legislature's law-making or executive action; vi) the existence, protection, and preservation of a "public sphere" that is independent from govern-ment, which may act as a space for public deliberation, as well as a space for holding government accountable.[10]

Constitutions, then, establish governments that are self-limiting and subordinate to "popular sovereignty," while also ensuring that no part of the people subordinate others of its parts. Constitutions also bind "popular sovereignty" and thus, one may argue, they are counter-majoritarian. To quote James Madison, from "Federalist 51":

> If men were angels, no government would be necessary. If angels were to govern men, neither external nor internal controls on government would be necessary. In framing a government which is to be administered by men over men, the great difficulty lies in this: you must first enable the government to control the governed; and in the next place oblige it to control itself. A dependence on the people is, no doubt, the primary control on the government; but experience has taught mankind the necessity of auxiliary precautions.[11]

Constitutional governments derive their power from the will of the people, and to that extent they are always limited by it; but constitu-tional governments also limit the will of the people by protecting them against themselves. Constitutions, then, generate, allocate, and limit political power by subordinating it to the rule of law, a rule that remains expansive and unspecified, for the constitution must also defer to the jurisgenesis of the courts.

Madison's "Federalist 51" is probably one of the best sources for understanding the virtues of constitutions *tout court*. Madison, Alexander Hamilton, and John Jay undoubtedly contributed to "per-suading" the American people of the virtues of their constitution. It is important to note that the ratification of that constitution came only after a long and very public debate, which to this date remains exem-plary. As Robert A. Ferguson argues in the introduction to his edition of *The Federalist*, the affirmation and celebration of the virtues of the proposed US Constitution make up one of the "greatest American contributions to world literature."[12] Indeed, it is fascinating to contemplate "constitutional debates" as contributions to world literature, as exercises in great rhetoric, but also as inspirations of both legal and moral imagination. For, ultimately, what constitutions aim at is establishing just, equitable, and self-limiting political orders, or what Plato called *Kallipolis*.

The US Constitution underwent a process of state ratification between 1787 and 1788, but it was not until 1791 that its first ten amendments were ratified, thus further delimiting a government that was already constituted as self-limiting. It is important to underscore that every constitution is, whether explicitly or implicitly, amendable. Every constitution has unleashed the power of constitutionalization through the process of constitutional amendments. To this day, the US Constitution has been amended twenty-seven times, as recently as 1992 (ratifying an amendment first proposed in 1789!). Constitutions, it may be argued, unleash not only jurisgenesis but also something that we can call constitutional pedagogy, or perhaps better, the pedagogy of law itself. It bears highlighting that the US Constitution was amended most expansively and radically after the American Civil War: with the thirteenth amendment, which abolished slavery; the fourteenth, which constitutionalized birthright citizenship; and the fifteenth, which extended and secured voting right to all citizens. The premier historian of the American Civil War and its aftermath, the Reconstruction, has called these amendments a "second founding" of the republic and a "remaking" of the constitution.[13] It must be noted that while the constitution was remade with these post–civil-war amendments, it would take almost another hundred years for the promises of those amendments to transform the polity. It took another half a century, for instance, for the nineteenth amendment to be ratified – the amendment that in many ways corrected the bad semantics of the fifteenth, which did not specify that the right to vote would not be denied or abridged on the basis of sex or gender.

Another indispensable source for understanding the virtues of constitutions, in general, is Thomas Paine, who, shortly after the US Constitution was ratified, took stock of the accomplishments of that constitution, which it may be argued are the virtues of constitutions wherever they are written and ratified. Writing in 1791 his *Rights of Man*, which has the almost-never-mentioned subtitle

"Being an Answer to Mr. Burke's Attack on the French Revolution,"
Paine summarizes:

> A constitution is a thing *antecedent* to a government, and a gov-
> ernment is only the creature of a constitution. The constitution of
> a country is not the act of its government, but of the people con-
> stituting a government. It is the body of elements to which they
> can refer, and quote article by article, and which contain the prin-
> ciples on which the government shall be established, the manner
> in which it shall be organized, the powers it shall have, the mode
> of elections, the duration of parliaments, or by what other name
> such bodies may be called, the powers which the executive part of
> the government shall have; and, in fine, every thing that relates
> to the complete organization of a civil government, and the prin-
> ciples on which it shall act, and by which it shall be bound.[14]

Later, in Part Two of the *Rights of Man*, Paine will add: "A constitution is not the act of a government, but of a people constituting a
government, and government without a constitution is power without
a right."[15]

It is important to make explicit what Paine is claiming: first, that a
constitution is "antecedent," that is prior, to government; second, that
government and constitution are different; third, that constitutions
delegate and authorize different parts of the government, and most
important, a government that acts beyond those limits, that is, beyond
its legitimate authority, exercises "power" and not "authority." As
Ernst-Wolfgang Böckenförde, German legal scholar and former constitutional judge in Germany's Federal Constitutional Court, put it:
"It is a legal hallmark of the constitutional state in this sense that
within it there no longer exists an authority that is the holder of sovereignty. Every state organ stands *beneath* the constitution, is a
pouvoir constitué. It holds only those powers and competences granted
by the constitution."[16] The "constitution" is the *pouvoir constituant*,
the fount and source of all political authority and thus, *avant la
constitution ce n'est rien*.[17] To this extent, the constitution is its *phar-
makon* – its cure, but also its poison. We can face what has been called
"constitutional failure" (as the need for a nineteenth amendment, for
instance, demonstrated) but as most constitutions have shown, they
can be amended, and thus a new legitimate order can be brought into
life through jurisgenesis.[18]

CONSTITUTIONAL DECONSTRUCTIONS
AND FORGING COMMON FUTURES

Thus far I have described in broad strokes, with reference to the US Constitution (which, notwithstanding its many failing and betrayals, remains exemplary), the power of constitutionalism, as both a descriptive and normative project. I would like to harness that power by rephrasing one of Immanuel Kant's most memorable paragraphs, from the conclusion to his *Critique of Practical Reason*: "Two things fill the mind with ever new and increasing admiration and reverence, the more often and more steadily one reflects on them: *the starry heavens above me and the moral law within me.*"[19] My rephrasing would be: "Two things fill the mind with ever increasing admiration and reverence, the more often we reflect on them: the imponderable mystery of the cosmos and the rule of law that guides us in our fashioning a common future." Just as the moral law is admirable, more admirable is the law that we impose upon ourselves as peoples bound by constitutions. Now, I want to turn to what I will call the defetishizing and de-mystifying force of constitutions, which I also would like to call "constitutional deconstructions." I will describe five such deconstructions.

The first deconstruction is of the constitution itself. Every constitution is both a written text and an implied constitution, or what has been called the metaconstitution.[20] The written constitution is beholden to the norm of the rule of law and the supreme imperative to protect the rights of citizens, and this means that its catalogue of rights is always underspecified and inexhaustible. Constitutionalism, in its descriptive and normative senses, then, turns out to also be meta-constitutionalism.[21] The written constitution is a placeholder, so to speak, for the constitution that we are still writing. Every constitution is in an ongoing dialogue with its government, people, laws, and its own text. We can thus speak with Michelman of dialogic constitutionalism.[22]

The second deconstruction is of the state. What constitutions constitute are not monolithic states, with political power radiating from a Hobbesian/Benthamian tower of sovereignty, but horizontally divided branches of "government." Constitutions constrain and domesticate political power by dismembering the state into separate branches of government. Under a constitution it is not possible to proclaim either "I am the state" or "I am the law." To this extent, constitutional states are constitutional governments that are ceaselessly deconstructing and re-creating sovereignty.[23] Constitutional states are *de jure* and *de facto* administrative states.[24]

The third deconstruction is that of law. Law is not simply what is enacted and legislated; it is also that which stands the test of the rule of law and judicial review. Constitutions affirm the law, but do not sacralize positive law. In this sense, constitutionalism is a critique of legal positivism and the affirmation and endorsement of legal constructivism. Constitutionalism is jurisgenesis guided by the moral intent of the rule of law, and not a sacralizing or fetishizing of the law.[25]

The fourth deconstruction is that of right. In the same way and to the same extent that constitutions proclaim that law is law that is always in the making, rights are not what is spelled out in their texts but what remains to be juridified. Constitutional rights, in fact, are both under-determined and under-specified.[26] Constitutions claim no rights without law, and law is above all at the service of those rights specified – and those yet to be specified – in the constitution that we are called to continue writing. Constitutional law is always the unmaking of law in the name of the rule of law and the rights of citizens.

The fifth deconstruction is that of the "people." Constitutions are written in the name of the people, for the people, by the people – to paraphrase Abraham Lincoln – but also "beyond the people." Constitutions are written, not in the name of a past people, or present people, past generations or the present generation, but in the name of the "people to come," the future generations.[27] The constitution, though written in the name of the "people," does not belong to a "people." The US Constitution, for example, was written only by slave-owning, property-holding, white, and educated males. But this same constitution was taken and transformed by former slaves, women, ethnic, and non-binary-gender citizens. As the constitution deconstructs the written constitution, the state, law, and right, it opens up the very question of "who is the people?" to demystification. Under a constitution it is not possible to proclaim: "This is my country" ... "my government" ... "my constitution." For the constitution does not belong to those who wrote it, amended it, or continue to celebrate it as "a work of practical genius."[28] At the most, one can love it, behold it, celebrate it, and defend it.

To conclude: constitutions deconstruct some of the most obdurate and blindly worshipped fetishes of modern societies: the people, law, rights, the "state," and even the "written" constitution itself. They are able to do so because constitutions are jurisgenerative and thus temporal devices that bind societies across time by accumulating intergenerational legal and constitutional capital. The constitution is thus also the school of the people. One of the primary functions of a constitution is to ensure the staggered and disaggregated allocation of power: each branch of government has its own duration and its time of selection. Constitutions organize political power in a chronological form.[29] In the United States, for instance, presidents are elected every four years (limited to two terms); Congress, made up by the Senate (every six years, with one third of the senate elected or re-elected every two years); and the House of Representatives (every two years), as well as the Supreme Court (life-term appointments). Constitutions are, in fact, more than chronological devices; they valorize and organize political time. To paraphrase Ronald Dworkin's concluding sentences from his *Law's Empire*, constitutions as an orientation are:

> constructive: [they aim], in the interpretative spirit, to lay principle over practice to show the best route to a better future, keeping the right faith with the past. [They are] finally, a fraternal [filial] attitude, an expression of how we are united in community though divided in project, interest, and conviction. That is, anyway, what [a constitution] is for us: for the people we want to be and the community we aim to have.[30]

The argument has been that constitutions construct a pedestal from which we all, and those who will come and whom we do not yet know, will speak, make claims, present arguments, and assert allegations. They will have a voice so long as they grant the same right, platform, and court of appeal to those who – naked, poor, hungry, children of former slaves, immigrants, and refugees – will also make appeals and cry for a voice. Thus, the children of our children, whose claims we cannot anticipate, can also ascend and speak out from the pedestal of the law. That is how those without voices will be able to speak out.

NOTES

1 Martha Minow, Michael Ryan, and Austin Sarat, eds., *Narrative, Violence, and the Law: The Essays of Robert Cover* (Ann Arbor: University of Michigan Press, 1992), 96.

2 The congressional committee in charge of investigating the January 6 insurrection has been slowly releasing documents. Although it is too early to tell what happened and did not happen, it is already evident that there was a very concerted effort to overturn the democratic will of the people. Heather Cox Richardson, a history professor turned blogger, has provided the most in-depth, sustained, and extensive analysis of the committee's findings thus far. See her blog, *Letters from an American*. The archive can be found at: https://heathercoxrichardson.substack.com/archive.

3 Minow, Ryan, and Sarat, *Narrative, Violence, and the Law*, 95.

4 Alexander Somek, *The Cosmopolitan Constitution* (Oxford: Oxford University Press, 2014).

5 Alexander Hamilton, James Madison, and John Jay, *The Federalist* (New York: Barnes and Noble Classics, 2006), 9. I quote here from "Federalist 1."

6 Frank Michelman, "Law's Republic," *Yale Law Journal* 97, no. 8 (July 1988): 1499.

7 Mark E. Brandon, "Constitutionalism," in *The Oxford Handbook of the U.S. Constitution*, ed. Mark Tushnet, Mark A. Graber, and Sanford Levinson (Oxford: Oxford University Press, 2015), 763.

8 See for instance Jon E. Lewis, ed., *The Birth of Freedom* (New York: Gramercy Books, 2006), previously published as *A Documentary History of Human Rights*.

9 Dieter Grimm, *Constitutionalism: Past, Present, and Future* (Oxford: Oxford University Press, 2016), 3.

10 Brandon, "Constitutionalism," 763.

11 Hamilton, Madison, and Jay, *The Federalist*, 288.

12 Ibid., xiii.

13 Eric Foner, *The Second Founding: How the Civil War and Reconstruction Remade the Constitution* (New York: W.W. Norton, 2019).

14 Thomas Paine, *Collected Writings*, ed. Eric Foner (New York: Library of America, 1995), 467–8.

15 Ibid., 572.

16 Ernst-Wolfgang Böckenförde, *Constitutional and Political Theory: Selected Writings* 1 (Oxford: Oxford University Press, 2017), 143.

17 Ibid., 147.

18 Mark E. Brandon, *Free in the World: American Slavery and Constitutional Failure* (Princeton: Princeton University Press, 1998).

19 Immanuel Kant, *Practical Philosophy: The Cambridge Edition of the Works of Immanuel Kant*, trans. Mary J. Gregor, with a general introduction by Allen Wood (Cambridge: Cambridge University Press, 1996), 269. Italics in this translation.

20 Larry Alexander, ed., *Constitutionalism: Philosophical Foundations* (Cambridge: Cambridge University Press, 2001), 2–3.

21 See Gunther Teubner, *Constitutional Fragments: Societal Constitutionalism and Globalization* (Oxford: Oxford University Press, 2012), 153.

22 Michelman, "Law's Republic," 1493–537.

23 See Böckenförde, *Constitutional and Political Theory*, 145.

24 Cass R. Sunstein and Adrian Vermeule, *Law and Leviathan: Redeeming the Administrative State* (Cambridge: Belknap Press of Harvard University Press, 2020).

25 Ronald Dworkin, *Freedom's Law: The Moral Reading of the American Constitution* (Cambridge: Harvard University Press, 1996).

26 See Dan Edelstein, *On the Spirit of Rights* (Chicago and London: University of Chicago Press, 2019), chapter VI: "Natural Constitutionalism and American Rights."

27 For a deconstruction of the "aporetic" status of the people both in the Declaration of Independence and in the Constitution see Jacques Derrida, "Declarations of Independence," in *Negotiations: Interventions and Interviews, 1971–2001,* ed. Jacques Derrida (Stanford: Stanford University Press, 2002), 46–54, as well as Michelman, "Constitutional Authorship," in *Constitutionalism: Philosophical Foundations*, ed. Larry Alexander (Cambridge: Cambridge University Press, 2001), 64–98.

28 Danielle Allen, "The Constitution Counted My Great-Great-Grandfather as Three-Fifths of a Free Person. He Is Why I Love It Anyway," *The Atlantic* 326, no. 3, October 2020, 58–63. Citation at page 63, right column.

29 See Grimm, *Constitutionalism,*18. The best treatments I have read of this theme, however, are Elizabeth F. Cohen, *The Political Value of Time: Citizenship, Duration, and Democratic Justice* (Cambridge: Cambridge University Press, 2018), 71–82, and Robert Cover's essay "Nomos and Narrative" in *Narrative, Violence, and the Law: The Essays of Robert Cover*, eds. Martha Minow, Michael Ryan, and Austin Sarat (Ann Arbor: University of Michigan Press, 1992), 95–172.

30 Ronald Dworkin, *Law's Empire* (Cambridge and London: The Belknap Press of Harvard University Press, 1986), 413.

4

Direct Democracy

Francesco Pallante

In its pure form, democracy implies a coincidence between those who make decisions on political organization (the rulers) and those who have to obey their determinations (the ruled). Indeed, obeying the law and acting according to the law means acting according to one's own will. Ultimately, the democratic ideal is an ideal of self-government, and its realization is the fulfilment of the human aspiration for freedom: here lies the appeal of direct democracy.

From this perspective, a democracy, to be considered as such, has to be direct: if the *demos* (the people) does not hold the *kratos* (power), then there is no democracy. The people's assembly, which acts potentially with the involvement of all the citizens, is the democratic instrument par excellence. The experiences of classical Athens and the Paris Commune – examples from ancient and modern history – still serve as powerful ideal references of a people's assembly. Nevertheless, in contemporary constitutions, this institution has nearly disappeared: evidence of it can be found only in two small Swiss cantons – Appenzell Innerrhoden and Glarus – and in San Marino. Nowadays, the most widespread instruments of direct democracy are the *referendum*, the popular legislative initiative, the *recall*, the popular petition, and the primary elections. However, far from ensuring the people's continuous contribution in all political decisions, these forms of direct participation of citizens in democratic decision-making involve only occasional participation and involve only specific issues. On closer inspection, they presuppose an institutional system of the parliamentary type within which they can operate as possible correctives.

The opposite of democracy is representation, as emerges historically from the contrast between the ideas of Rousseau[1] and Montesquieu.[2] Representation implies a distinction, not a coincidence, between the rulers and the ruled: the representatives make decisions; the represented obey. There is no necessary implication of coincidence between representation and democracy, since kings have always presented themselves as representatives of the people. Even after the French Revolution and until the introduction of the universal suffrage – male and female – parliamentary representation was not democratic.

Thus, democratic representation – or representative democracy – is a synthesis of two opposing ideals: all the governed directly choose their rulers; hence, a representative system is all the more democratic when: (*a*) electoral law is proportional (and not majoritarian); (*b*) there is a coincidence between the governed and the voters (and consequently, political rights depend on residency, not on citizenship).

* * *

The impracticability of direct democracy in mass societies has long justified the choice of representation. However, today's information technology revolution has opened up new perspectives. The primary forms of social mediation of the twentieth century have suffered an overall devaluation. In particular, different aspects of the broader phenomenon of disintermediation[3] – trade unions, for instance, the education system, the media, medicine, science, and even parties, traditional instruments of political intermediation – have undergone a crisis of disavowal in favour of individual and immediate political action[4]

This phenomenon reached its peak worldwide with the triumph of the Five Star Movement in the 2018 Italian elections. However, its origin can be symbolically traced back to the political adventure undertaken in the United States almost thirty years ago by Ross Perot. The idea was to build a telematic network connecting every American citizen directly and continuously to the federal government. Thanks to this disruptive approach, Perot obtained 19 per cent of the vote in the presidential elections in 1992, becoming the most successful independent candidate in recent history.

Analysis of concrete experiments such as Germany's Piraten (Pirate Party) shows that virtual tools do not facilitate political participation; on the contrary, they reinforce the dynamics of real-life situations.[5] That is demonstrated by the phenomenon of so-called echo-chambers; that is, the structuring of social media in closed environments whereby users continuously receive confirmation of their (pre)judgments by interacting exclusively with people who have the same ideas.[6]

In particular, two considerations reveal the nature of the Internet. In the first place, every individual is exposed to an overload of information. As calculated in 2008, people are "bombarded" every day with at least 100,000 words, far more than our brains can process. Having too many elements available hinders concentration and diverts our attention toward information more likely to evoke strong emotions and less complex to process. Indeed, we confront a paradox: information overload reduces the ability to process it but increases the need to make decisions. The result is that more and more people rely on algorithms, without exploiting their real potential: who goes beyond the first page of the results of a Google search?[7]

The second consideration can be traced back to those who, as Evgeny Morozov describes, take advantage of the naivety of contemporary individuals, who, intending to defend their freedom, end up entrusting themselves to private companies that pursue their own commercial interests by exploiting users' personal data.[8] It is an acute criticism that allows us to reformulate the objection of the impracticability of direct democracy. How much freedom do social media permit us to express? Which unconscious influences record, classify, and cross-reference our preferences? Who finds, selects, and prioritizes information online? Furthermore, how is the process performed? These questions narrow the "revolutionary" scope of the ongoing technological transformations.

* * *

Donald Trump's rise to the presidency of the United States is emblematic of the meaning of doing politics through the Internet. Twitter, Facebook, and other social networks proved to be perfect tools for someone who, after falsely claiming to be an anti-system outsider and demonizing the traditional media, built his enormous political consensus on establishing a direct relationship with his followers.

The Cambridge Analytica scandal cost Facebook a five-billion-dollar fine, the highest ever imposed on a computer company by the Federal Trade Commission. It revealed how sophisticated the manipulation of users' online traces for profiling purposes can be. Classifying potential supporters and opponents with accuracy, especially in swing constituencies, in order to encourage the former and discourage the latter from voting, and knowing what beliefs, ideals, needs, concerns, and fears might lead them to decide one way or the other, proved to give an extraordinary competitive advantage for Trump. The social networks themselves have largely benefited, as tens of millions of people who saw Trump as a symbol to identify with quickly became followers of his accounts.

The war on traditional media, conducted in an unscrupulous manner by the former president, proved in turn to be perfectly useful to his objective of accrediting himself as a well-meaning common person, opposed by organized powers (the so-called "Deep State") subservient to the interests of the enemies of the people. Whoever they may be – pedophiles, homosexuals, feminists, Blacks, Jews, Muslims, Hispanics, communists, Russians, Chinese, scientists – everyone is fair game for conspiracy theorists, even Hugo Chavez or Fidel Castro, even though they have been dead for years. This trend represents a trap for newspapers and television stations: in order to recover the users they have lost, they have to shift from analogue to digital. However, in so doing, they become perfect targets for those who consider them useful instruments for manipulating public opinion and reinforcing hostile convictions in an atmosphere of increasingly extreme polarization.

This situation explains the ease with which Donald Trump convinced his most enthusiastic followers to storm the Capitol. Everything had been ready for some time, like a spring-loaded mechanism that only needed to be triggered. What better trigger than the leader himself – perhaps, more correctly, the *duce* – who, addressing each of his followers directly, invokes their help against those who, with trickery and subterfuge, would like to put them all out of the game in one fell swoop?

* * *

The real shortcoming of direct democracy is not practical but conceptual. As Norberto Bobbio maintained, "nothing kills democracy more than an excess of democracy."[9] The meaning is evident: public institutions cannot operate by constantly submitting to the people decisions that cause social division. Universal suffrage determines the recognition and the affirmation of pluralism and diversity in contemporary societies, which require the careful and constant search for solutions of balance, in order to allow different political, economic, and cultural components to coexist peacefully. Indeed, the never-quite-dormant risk of political unity's dissolution into fratricidal plurality needs to be kept under control.[10] As Giovanni Sartori argues, while direct democracy, seeing "politics as war," triggers a "zero-sum" game in which "whoever wins, wins all; whoever loses,

loses everything," representative democracy, seeing "politics as negotiation," produces a "positive-sum" game in which, thanks to mediation, everyone gains something.[11]

Hence, the principal theorist of twentieth-century democracy, Hans Kelsen, emphasized the primacy of the deliberative moment – that is discussion – over decision-making.[12] Democracy functions above all through discussion, not through choice. Ideally, decision-making is a resource to be used as a last resort, when all other attempts to create consensus fail. A democrat is someone who openly confronts others; from his own convictions, he or she looks forward to a compromise capable of recognizing the value of other people's convictions. Ultimately, the mere counting of votes does not produce democratic decisions, but rather impositions of partisanship. That is even more evident when, in the parliamentary sphere, the distribution of seats is conditioned by the manipulation of electoral results in a disproportional manner.

A decision taken directly by the people, even by computer vote, cannot therefore be considered genuinely democratic. The mere numerical composition of individual preferences does not build bridges between the different components of society; on the contrary, it builds walls. A system of this sort represents the tyranny of the majority, not democracy. Only through public discussion can personal opinions cease to be idiosyncrasies and become comparable in view of thought-out decisions supported by broad consensus.[13] As Gustavo Zagrebelsky wrote, "in order for the law not to be violent and, therefore, not to contradict the very idea of law ... it is necessary to persuade the other party, the one that did not participate in determining the content of the deliberation."[14] This requires, at the very least, a sincere attempt at persuasion.

* * *

The Trilateral Commission's well-known 1975 report on the "excess of democracy" in Western societies[15] was precisely against this concept. The report, presented in conjunction with the explosion of the fiscal crisis of the state, revolved around the thesis that parliamentary democracy had gone too far in its efforts to satisfy citizens' numerous demands for protection; the tax burden on the richest had grown disproportionately, taking resources away from the free unfolding of economic dynamics.

In order to free up these resources and give the capitalist economy a new lease on life, the report suggested, the role of the state vis-à-vis society needed to be questioned. Subsidiarity was the watchword; the collective space must open to a plurality of possible interventions. The public sector, it claimed, had no primacy. On the contrary, it should only be entitled to act on a subsidiary level if society is unable to provide for itself in its various forms.

The concept of the subsidiary state developed along two lines: loosening the grip of the state on civil society and bringing institutions closer to citizens. The common denominator is their critique of the artificiality of intermediate bodies in favour of the naturalness of relations directly entertained through the market. This applies to horizontal relations between private and private and, in the case of vertical relations between private and public, through the network.

In recent decades, the first aspect has been based on harnessing the individual potentialities set free by the hypertrophy of the public sector. In particular, we have seen the contraction of the state's role in the economy through privatization and liberalization; regulatory reduction and simplification; the abolition of public funding for political parties and the liberalization of private funding; the reduction or the dismantling of many public services; the corporatization of the remaining ones (particularly health and social services); and the transformation of public action into an activity negotiated between citizens and public administration. As a backdrop to these politics is governance – a theory of horizontal, diffuse, contractualized power.

In the second place – inspired by the idea of making citizens protagonists of a new era of participation – worldwide transformations have shifted the core of the constitutional orders from parliamentary assemblies to executive bodies and, consequently, from organized political formations to individual leaders able to enter into direct relationship with voters. As an immediate consequence, party structures have been dismantled; political contention has been personalized; the primaries, means for selecting the ruling class, have been abused; the programs of different political sides have been merged. Nevertheless, political compromise (personal loyalties are not negotiable) has been scorned and the free parliamentary mandate has been criticized, if not attacked – up to the point of it being considered normal for political minorities, artificially swollen into parliamentary majorities by the manipulation of electoral systems, to govern complex and plural contemporary societies. The common background is the theme of governability: a theory of vertical, concentrated, decision-making power.

So we have *governance* and *governability*: two different theories of power, sharing the common aim of fostering the role of individuals, bringing their interests into public discussion (governance), or directly choosing leaders and substantive policy lines (governability).

* * *

Paradoxically, the dismantling of structured political formations – with a strong anti-*establishment* connotation, in the name of the citizen's sovereignty – has lately exacerbated the oligarchic tendency of political systems. Parties, deprived of activists and ideals, have lost their ability to act as instruments of mediation between society and institutions. They have turned into electoral cartels aimed at conquering power on behalf of narrow governing circles. Indeed, from the perspective of these circles, parties never had so much power: they structure political competition, conduct electoral campaigns, select elected political staff, and appoint the holders of government posts and all other public offices.[16]

If we look more closely, we see that the political proposal that most proclaims itself to be a break with the past – the one inspired by direct democracy – is, in reality, extraordinarily conformist to it. From the denial of political ideologies to the rejection of party organization; from the reduction in the number of representatives to the criticism of free parliamentary mandate; from the celebration of civil society to the rejection of professional political commitment; from the intolerance of controlling institutions to the strengthening of the referendum institute: all the proposed measures tend to increase direct and widespread popular involvement in political decisions, to the detriment of traditional party forms of mediation.

There is one constant that characterizes these phenomena: the idea that all individuals know what is preferable for them. It is the rhetoric of individual sovereignty, carved into the collective memory by Margaret Thatcher's lie: "society does not exist; only individuals exist." In reality, far from valuing individuals, this vision leads to the creation of a community of isolated subjects left to their own devices. Kelsen himself anticipated the risks of breaking down society into individual monads:

It is a well-known fact that, because he is unable to achieve any appreciable influence on government, the isolated individual lacks any real political existence. Democracy is only feasible if, in order to influence the will of society, individuals integrate themselves into associations based on their various political goals. Collective bodies, which unite the common interests of their individual members as political parties, must come to mediate between the individual and the state.

From this perspective, he added, "there can be no serious doubt that efforts ... to discredit political parties both theoretically and juristically constituted an ideologically veiled resistance to the realization of democracy."[17] Sharing the same view, Robert Michels observed that "democracy is inconceivable without organization" and added that organization "is the weapon given to the weak in the struggle against the strong, a struggle that can only be developed on the terrain of solidarity between associates."[18] This is exactly what terrified Margaret Thatcher: that the weakest would draw strength from their union.

* * *

Finally, political representation remains an irreplaceable tool: insofar as they are called upon to represent the nation in its entirety, and not small groups of voters who elected them, only representatives can set themselves the objective of building consensus by identifying and realizing the general interest. Anyone else could only act in a private capacity; that is, letting their own particular interest prevail over others, even if it is supported by a numerical majority.

The presence of collective entities such as parties remains an essential instrument of political and social integration. Indeed, parties are bearers of one of many possible worldviews proposed to society as desirable political ideals. They can make available to their members a "political capital" competitive with people who have their own economic and cultural resources. However, parties are structured in internal representative bodies, putting the base in two-way communication with the top. If able to interpret their role correctly, parties operate as parts that address the whole; that is, as subjects intrinsically open to compromise. In this way, while competing with each other, they operate as instruments of unification of a social body that is increasingly varied and in danger of being torn apart. As Kelsen, again, wrote: "compromise is part of democracy's very nature." In addition: "insofar as in a democracy the contents of the legal order, too, are not determined exclusively by the interests of the majority, but are the result of a compromise between two groups, voluntary subjection of all individuals to the legal order is more easily possible than in any other political organization."[19]

This is the benchmark. Direct democracy fascinates because it gives us the illusion that we can be governed by ourselves. In reality, it exposes us to the risk of domination by an opposing majority. Representative democracy protects us from this risk, because it is the only system capable of producing collective decisions in such a way that they are "the result of the maximum of critical consensus and the minimum of imposition."[20] If the democratic crisis stems from the failure to involve citizens in decisions that affect them, direct democracy, far from being the cure, risks embodying its most acute and conclusive phase.

NOTES

1 Jean-Jacques Rousseau (1762), *The Social Contract*, Book III, chapter 15.
2 Montesquieu (1762), *The Spirit of Laws*, 1748, Book II, chapter 2, and Book XI, chapter 6.
3 Andrew Chadwick, "Disintermediation," in *Sage Encyclopedia of Governance*, eds. Mark Bevir et al. (London: Sage, 2006), 232–3.
4 Moreover, the criticism of political parties – as electoral machines at the service of politicians interested not in the welfare of the electorate but in grabbing public office – can be traced back at least to Joseph A. Schumpeter, *Capitalism, Socialism and Democracy* (New York: Harper & Brothers, 1942).
5 Carsten Koschmieder, "Do More Opportunities for Participation Imply More Democracy? The Case of the German Pirate Party," *Teoría Política*, no. 5 (2015): 32.
6 Walter Quattrociocchi, Antonio Scala, and Cass R. Sunstein, "Echo Chambers on Facebook," *John M. Olin Center for Law, Economics, and Business Discussion Paper*, no. 877 (2016).
7 Ninety-five per cent of computer searches worldwide – over one hundred billion per month – go through Google. Fewer than one in ten users go

beyond the first page of search results, and two out of three *clicks* focus on the first three entries: https://www.advancedwebranking.com/ctrstudy/.

8 Evgeny Morozov, *The Net Delusion: The Dark Side of Internet Freedom* (New York: PublicAffairs, 2011). And Evgeny Morozov, *To Save Everything, Click Here: The Folly of Technological Solutionism* (New York: PublicAffairs, 2013).

9 Norberto Bobbio, "Democrazia rappresentativa e democrazia diretta," in *Democrazia e partecipazione,* ed. Guido Quazza Turin: Stampatori, 1978), 19–46.

10 Obvious references are the classics Thomas Hobbes, *Leviathan* (Berkeley: University of California Press, 1652); and Max Weber, *Economy and Society* (Berkeley: University of California Press, 1978).

11 Giovanni Sartori, "Tecniche decisionali e sistema dei comitati," in *Rivista Italian di Scienza Politica,* no. 1 (1974), 22, 40.

12 Hans Kelsen, *The Essence and Value of Democracy,* edited by Nadia Urbinati and Carlo Invernizzi Accetti and translated by Brian Graf, Lanham: Rawman & Littlefield, 2013 (orig. ed. 1929) and Hans Kelsen, *Das Problem des parlamentarismus* (W. Braumüller, Vienna-Leipzig, 1924).

13 Carl Schmitt had already argued this almost a century ago, in Carl Schmitt, *Constitutional Theory,* trans. Jeffrey Seitzer (Durham: Duke University Press, 2008).

14 Gustavo Zagrebelsky, *Intorno alla legge. Il diritto come dimensione del vivere comune* (Turin: Einaudi, 2009), 27.

15 Michael Crozier, Samuel P. Huntington, and Joji Watanuki, *The Crisis of Democracy: Report on the Governability of Democracies to the Trilaterial Commission* (New York: New York University Press, 1975).

16 Alfio Mastropaolo, "Crisi dei partiti o decadimento della democrazia," *Constituzionalismo.it,* 23 May 2005, https://www.costituzionalismo.it/crisi-dei-partiti-o-decadimento-della-democrazia/.

17 Kelsen, *The Essence and Value of Democracy,* 39.

18 Robert Michels, *La sociologia del partito politico nella democrazia moderna* (Bologna: il Mulino, 1966, orig. ed. 1911).

19 Hans Kelsen, *General Theory of Law and State* (New Brunswick, NJ, and London: Transaction Publications, 2006, orig. ed. 1945), 288.

20 Michelangelo Bovero, *Contro il governo dei peggiori. Una grammatica della democrazia* (Rome-Bari: Laterza, 2000), 54–5.

5

The Prosecution Project:
Data-Driven Anti-fascism in a Post-truth, Proto-fascist Era

Michael Loadenthal

[Fascism] is therefore a spiritual conception, itself also a result of the general reaction of the Century against the languid and materialistic positivism of the Eighteenth Century. Anti-positivist, but positive: neither skeptical nor agnostic.[1]

Benito Mussolini, 1927

THINKING ABOUT A REVOLUTION

As a youth, when I daydreamed of fighting the forces of domination and control, I saw myself draped in dusty bandoliers, shouldering a wooden-stocked Soviet-era rifle, and speaking in coded communications through handheld radios and secret earpieces. In my mind's eye I resembled the EZLN's Subcomandante Marcos, Spanish anarcho-anti-fascist Buenaventura Durruti, or Nestor Makhno of the Black Army, galloping on horseback throughout Ukraine. Now, more than two decades into a life as an organizer, trainer, and researcher among dissident resistance movements challenging the far right, I see more and more that alongside every combatant is a heap of knowledge, and beneath that, data.

Though it disappoints a younger me to replace Semtex with spreadsheets, and RPGs with Restricted Data Use Agreements, in the post-truth, "science-doesn't-know" era we find ourselves in, to champion empiricism can be an oddly revolutionary and anti-statist posture.

Figure 5.1 "For Every Fighter There Are 10+ Supports."

It is essential in the fight against the fascist creep[2] that marked the first year of the global COVID-19 health pandemic, which reached a dramatic climax on 6 January 2021, with the siege of the US Capitol. This insurrectionary attack was itself a contestation of established, data-driven facts. The insurrectionists doubted the results of the 2020 presidential election and sought to intervene in the transfer of power by disrupting official proceedings. They were a mixture of "Make

America Great Again" and so-called Stop-the-Steal activists, Proud
Boys, militia, boogalooers, QAnon supporters, and a smattering
of white supremacist and other far-right adherents, urged on by a
petulant American president. The crowd was made up of a "disproportionate" number of current and former police and soldiers –
between 14 and 20 per cent of the crowd in a nation where they only
make up 6 to 7 per cent of the population.[3] The act was not unlike
earlier attempts by fascists to gain power, from Mussolini's 1922
march on Rome, to Hitler's 1923 Munich Beer Hall Putsch.

RECONCILING ROLES:
THE SECOND WORLD WAR AND J20

I am an anti-fascist. This is part of my heritage as a third-generation
American and an Ashkenazi Jew.

I entered this world, coincidentally, a century after Benito Mussolini,
yet I emerged via a decidedly oppositional lineage that included two
grandfathers who left their homes in Philadelphia to pursue Nazi
fascists in the "last great war." The heroic fight against Hitler, "Il
Duce," and their allies was enshrined in notions of patriotism, bravery,
and sacrifice; and resultingly, the enemy were bemoaned as evil, however banal their cruelty was judged to be. The global awareness of the
embodied wickedness of Hitler's fascists drove my grandfathers –
Robert "Bob" Cohen, and Joseph "Duke" Loadenthal – to war. Duke's
widow once showed me a photograph her late husband had smuggled
out during the liberation of Buchenwald, one of Germany's first and
largest death camps. The photo, a frayed square containing a black
and white image, exhibited a pile of skulls, neatly stacked.

In my own dark era, an avowed rejection of xenophobic, misogynistic authoritarianism led me to the streets of Washington, DC, on
20 January 2017, with the intention of disrupting the coronation of
the republic's forty-fifth ruler, a man keen on winding the clocks
backward to around the era when my grandparents went to war.

As is a matter of public (court) record, on that cold January day, I
made the trek to Logan Circle, donned my balaclava, took to the
streets, and in short order found myself charged under federal indictment with hundreds of co-defendants. In the months that followed
my assault and capture, what began as a single felony quickly became
a forty-nine-page, fourteen-count indictment charging conspiracy,
incitement, destruction of property, assault while armed, and a host

of other crimes.[4] After nearly two years of prosecution, the state would unceremoniously drop the case against me, after finding itself unable to win even a single jury conviction among my many co-defendants.

As a scholar of political protest and violence, I was not new to the carceral state, its particularities or ideological asymmetries. I am well aware of the uneven sentences awarded to leftists when compared to white supremacists and (so-called) Salafi-Jihadists. After my arrest, when I was able to regain perspective on my own prosecution, I began to explore the data. What factors most influenced our treatment by the US Attorneys' Office and the Department of Justice? Was it our ideology? Our motive? Was it the demographics of the individuals involved? Was it something else? These questions led to a multi-year research program that still continues more than five years later.

THE PROSECUTION PROJECT

The Prosecution Project (tPP) is the platform I developed to dig into these questions. tPP's aim is to establish an empirical basis to discuss criminal sentencing trends and outliers, and to examine how a defendant's crime relates to their treatment within the justice system. As a social scientist – a self-taught sociologist and criminologist with four semi-related, interdisciplinary degrees – I am committed to justice and, in my leadership of tPP, I have sought to use the platform to decipher the intricate patterns created in the prosecution of political crime, and the development of an ideologically neutral means for interpreting state response.

What struck me about my own case was precisely how it constructed me as the subject, how it followed the "act of becoming" first a *dissident*, then a *rioter*, and then a *defendant*, and possibly, a *felon* and *prisoner*. In this act, there was an intermixing of subjectivities.

Queer theorist Jasbir Puar refers to this manner of assemblage, wherein the organic (body) combines with the inorganic (data) to foster a "data body."[5] In my case, this took the form of becoming another individual on a criminal docket, another entry in the electronic court system, another name constituting the collective "et al.," and another row in tPP. This act of *becoming* is a subtle metamorphosis from citizen to juridical subject.

As the project's director, I have the job of keeping tPP relevant and engaged; through design and methodological choices, my beliefs, assumptions, and epistemological peculiarities are reflected in the

Date	Date descriptor	Case ID	Group Identifier	Full legal name	First name	Family name	Other names/aliases	Co-offenders	Reason for inclusion
01/20/2017	Crime/attack	01202017_CC_J20-9	J20-9					Yes	Obvious socio-political aim AND State
01/20/2017	Crime/attack	01202017_KC_J20-10	J20-10					Yes	Obvious socio-political aim AND State
01/20/2017	Crime/attack	01202017_AC_J20-11	J20-11					Yes	Obvious socio-political aim AND State
01/20/2017	Crime/attack	01202017_EF_J20-12	J20-12					Yes	Obvious socio-political aim AND State
01/20/2017	Crime/attack	01202017_MG_J20-13	J20-13					Yes	Obvious socio-political aim AND State
01/20/2017	Crime/attack	01202017_LG_J20-14	J20-14					Yes	Obvious socio-political aim AND State
01/20/2017	Crime/attack	01202017_JMH_J20-15	J20-15					Yes	Obvious socio-political aim AND State
01/20/2017	Crime/attack	01202017_PH_J20-16	J20-16					Yes	Obvious socio-political aim AND State
01/20/2017	Crime/attack	01202017_PJ_J20-17	J20-17					Yes	Obvious socio-political aim AND State
01/20/2017	Crime/attack	01202017_SK_J20-18	J20-18					Yes	Obvious socio-political aim AND State
01/20/2017	Crime/attack	01202017_ML_J20-19	J20-19	Michael Loadenthal	Michael	Loadenthal	None	Yes	Obvious socio-political aim AND State
01/20/2017	Crime/attack	01202017_JL_J20-20	J20-20					Yes	Obvious socio-political aim AND State
01/20/2017	Crime/attack	01202017_DM2_J20-21	J20-21					Yes	Obvious socio-political aim AND State
01/20/2017	Crime/attack	01202017_RM_J20-22	J20-22					Yes	Obvious socio-political aim AND State
01/20/2017	Crime/attack	01202017_MRM_J20-23	J20-23					Yes	Obvious socio-political aim AND State
01/20/2017	Crime/attack	01202017_GWM_J20-24	J20-24					Yes	Obvious socio-political aim AND State

Figure 5.2 Prosecution Project data. Redacted screen grab of data created by author as executive director of the Prosecution Project.

variables that are measured, the value ranges assigned, and the determinations of whether to include or exclude borderline cases.[6] My role is to act as arbiter when the lines are fuzzy. Project teams follow the cadence and direction of a diverse milieu of terrorists, extremists, and those motivated to violence by bias, hate, and dissent. tPP follows the violence, the arrests, and the individuals prosecuted.

When we began in March 2017, we were rapidly coding cases involving a spike in white nationalist and so-called alt-right-driven violence. By summer 2020, our work had shifted to documenting Black Lives Matter and anti-police protestors, as their prosecutions had outpaced those of the far right. Several months later, by winter 2021, we were back to mostly coding right-wing cases as the state steadily rolled out hundreds of indictments[7] against Capitol insurrectionists.

This journey mirrors my own foci, as I have shifted my attention from domestic militias, to the Global War on (Salafi-Islamist-Jihadi) Terror, to the targeting of eco/animal liberation activists, and then at present, to those the state categorizes as rioters, anarchists, and "antifa" – the bogeyman of the 2020s. In the late 1990s, in light of the 1995 Oklahoma City bombing by Timothy McVeigh, I was fascinated with militias. Then, after the attacks on US embassies in Kenya and Tanzania, it was so-called Salafi-Jihadists. When friends began to be arrested in the early 2000s as part of the FBI-led counter-terrorism initiative known among activists as "the Green Scare," I widened my focus yet again.

This is to say that I have always followed the violence and adapted to what was engaging and relevant.

BATTLES FOR TRUTH

Scholarly efforts are often understood to be searches for truth. I began examining the presence of Aryan Nations in my Pennsylvania community as a youth because I wanted to challenge the notion that they were "racialists," and establish that they were instead violent bigots.[8] I investigated al-Qaeda and their contemporaries[9] in part to challenge the "they-hate-our-freedom" trope, and the notion that strikes against the United States lacked strategy and logic, despite Osama bin Laden's many pre-attack proclamations. I investigated eco-terrorism, spending much of my early career writing on this topic,[10] because I wanted to dispel the notion that activists' undertakings were characterized by terrorism, arguing rather that violence meant to evoke fear was exceedingly rare, atypical, and not emblematic of the movement's aims or means.

When I began TPP, I saw it as an extension of a legacy of data-driven truth-seeking. TPP emerged while the US president was denying the validity of science-driven approaches to understanding complex social phenomena, and our efforts have challenged this post-truth discursive regime through data-driven labour. When we began, historic cuts to government-aligned, empirically driven centres established to study terrorism and political violence were underway. The Global Terrorism Database, the most widely known, non-classified, public terrorism databank, was defunded after the State Department decided to put its money behind another, less transparent project that presented a bid 0.2 per cent lower.[11] This action would help to distinguish the forty-fifth president's anti-scientific framework.

He would go on to advocate obviously nativist policies based on false science,[12] and bemoan the media – even conservative media – as "fake news"[13] and "the enemy of the people."[14] Concurrent with these efforts and expanding throughout his administration, the president defunded programs established to understand, reduce, and counter extremism,[15] choosing to support programs described by the Brennan Center for Justice as "operat[ing] on the bizarre and unsupported assumption that diversity and the experience of discrimination in America are suggestive of a national security threat … that Muslim, immigrant, black or LGBTQ Americans, from kindergarten on, must be surveilled to keep our country safe."[16] Following the same twisted, politically driven logic, the president redirected resources *away* from countering the far right, the movement most linked to violence throughout his time in office.[17]

The aim of knowledge constructors should be to debate the interpretation, meaning, and trajectory of events, not their mere existence. Claims such as "most terrorists are foreign"[18] or "most rioters are outside agitators"[19] were both loudly and falsely made by the US president, and can be easily challenged with the data we have assembled and work to make widely available. The aforementioned threat to positivist science, truth, logic, and data was not restricted to understanding political violence. In September 2020, at a meeting with California secretary for natural resources Wade Crowfoot and other officials battling wildfires, the then-president was asked about the "warming trend" observed by climatologists and scientists. This exchange was recorded by White House transcript:

Crowfoot: I think we want to work with you [the president] to really recognize the changing climate and what it means to our forests and actually work together with that science, that science is going to be key, because if we ignore that science and put our head in the sand ... we're not going to succeed together protecting Californians.

President: Okay. It'll start getting cooler ... You just watch.

Crowfoot: I wish science agreed with you.

President: Well, I don't think science knows, actually.[20]

At that moment, in that one assertion of science's "unknowingness," we subtly crossed the Rubicon into a period of fascistic anti-intellectualism, our own Dark Ages 2.0.

While the use of the f-word may have appeared melodramatically premature in 2017, by 2021 even noted historian of fascism Robert Paxton remarked: "[The President's] encouragement of civic violence to overturn an election crosses a red line. The label [of fascist] now seems not just acceptable but necessary."[21] Fascism in its classical iteration is not only militarist, elitist, and nationalist; it is also inherently anti-liberal, anti-democratic, anti-Enlightenment, and anti-rational – oppositional to empiricism, intellect, and knowledge construction.[22] One of fascism's keen witnesses, Jewish philosopher Hannah Arendt, who chronicled the famed 1961 trial of Adolf Eichmann in Jerusalem, noted that fascist totalitarians regularly distorted the "factualness" of inquiry, presented their own faux-science as truth, and sought narrative control by delegitimizing and challenging scientific discourses.[23]

Thus, tPP emerged in a troubled time – a time when students were being taught to distrust science; when they were being told by the president that belief could trump fact. It was a time in which US intelligence agencies could all say one thing and the president another.[24] The desire to empirically measure complex socio-political phenomena was made necessary by the president, and tPP emerged from that chaos. A grasp to gain a foothold on meaning; a desperate reach upward toward science.

DECENTRALIZED CELLS OF ACADEMIC INSURGENTS

Despite its start nearly three years earlier, tPP was forged and solidified in the fires of the global coronavirus pandemic which forced many of us out of the classroom, and some of us out of a job. What began as a (more or less) traditional internship for enterprising undergraduates became a decentralized, globally dispersed research platform wherein, not unlike clandestine cells, teams of researchers function as self-contained units with limited command and control, combing through databanks to translate complex stories into qualitative codes suitable for aggregation. While the various "cells" communicate with one another when necessary, most act entirely autonomously, intentionally siloed, and blissfully unaware of what their co-conspirators are working on. While two researchers can spend weeks exploring a group of Michiganders plotting to kidnap the governor,[25] others explore New Englanders supporting the Islamic State,[26] or begin wading through indicted clusters of white supremacist gang members.[27]

At any given movement, more than thirty researchers dispersed throughout the United States and beyond are studying hundreds of cases simultaneously. Decentralization is a key guiding value for tPP, both for our research team structure and for the project's resulting knowledge. Decentralization legitimizes essential strategic choices when opposing authoritarianism and fascism.

Beyond decentralizing our structure and moving away from the constraints of synchronous, shared (physical) meeting spaces and institutional red tape, tPP embraces the scientific notion of replication – the ability to repeat another's study to verify, compare, and critique. tPP serves as a public-facing mirror for the often-opaque and difficult-to-navigate realities exposed through court records. By translating these documents into qualitative codes and data-driven narratives, we preserve the basic factuality of events for others to build upon. We work to foster and preserve the integrity of the data through continual audit and revision, providing the public the most accurate and complete information available at any given time. The preservation of this knowledge and history is key. Here, for instance, is one additional example.

On 20 January 2017, while I was kettled by police, the weather was dreary, rainy, cold, and unpleasant. The air was thick with the smell of tear gas, pepper spray, gun powder, and burning plastics. The presidential inauguration was taking place only a few blocks away; however, when asked to recall the day to members of the Central Intelligence Agency, the president said:

It was almost raining but God looked down and he said, we're not going to let it rain on your speech. In fact, when I first started, I said, oh, no. The first line, I got hit by a couple of drops. And I said, oh, this is too bad, but we'll go right through it. But the truth is that it stopped immediately. It was amazing. And then it became really sunny. And then I walked off and it poured right after I left. It poured.[28]

Yes, that would have been amazing, if it had happened. But it did not. It simply did not happen, and anyone present (or watching the video) knew that. Despite the outright falsehood, history becomes what we record it to be, and if one were to record the day's weather based on the president's memory, it was a sunny day. Thus, TPP serves as a public record, co-created by many eyes and hands.

In her foundational study of totalitarianism, Arendt notes that sloganeering jingoism – which crested violently when "MAGA"-adorned rioters stormed the US Capitol – is by its nature, anti-logic and irrational: "The curious logicality of all isms, their simple-minded trust in the salvation value of stubborn devotion without regard for specific, varying factors, already harbors the first germs of totalitarian contempt for reality and factuality."[29] This resistance to anti-factual "totalitarian contempt" is the reason TPP stands as a roadblock to fascism.

As an independent, ideologically neutral, non-partisan effort situated within an ethics of justice, transparency, and knowledge construction, the Prosecution Project is a platform that challenges fear-based, anti-scientific, and partisan portrayals of political violence summoned to validate a policy of securitization which serves to limit human freedoms through asymmetric police attention. Those of us who find ourselves in the digitally mediated trenches of our generation's Great War must build our foxholes deep and our ramparts tall if we are to summon the defensive force needed to find justice in increasingly fascistic times. Knowledge construction is an essential component of community self-defence, and it is within this politics that we tread onward, culling through an ever-growing caseload, and seeking to draw logical conclusions from a world that seems ever more illogical and unpredictable.

NOTES

1 Benito Mussolini, "The Doctrine of Fascism," in *Essays on Fascism* (London: Black House Publishing, 1927), 27.

2 This particular creep towards fascism was led by the forty-fifth US
   president, himself a proto-fascist, and an all-around creep.

3 Tom Dreisbach and Meg Anderson, "Nearly 1 in 5 Defendants in Capitol
   Riot Cases Served in the Military," *All Things Considered*, NPR,
   January 21, 2021, https://www.npr.org/2021/01/21/958915267/nearly-one-
   in-five-defendants-in-capitol-riot-cases-served-in-the-military; Sara Sidner,
   Anna-Maja Rappard, and Marshall Cohen, "Disproportionate Number
   of Current and Former Military Personnel Arrested in Capitol Attack,
   CNN Analysis Shows," CNN, 1 February 2021, https://www.cnn.com/
   2021/01/31/us/capitol-riot-arrests-active-military-veterans-soh/index.html.

4 Channing D. Phillips, *The United States of America* v. *Nathaniel H. Jaffe,
   et al., No. CF2 001147-CF2 001405.* Superior Court of the District of
   Columbia, 2017.

5 Jasbir Puar, *Terrorist Assemblages: Homonationalism in Queer Times*
   (Durham: Duke University Press, 2007), 175.

6 For a lengthy discussion of these methodological decisions, see: Michael
   Loadenthal, "Introducing the Prosecution Project 2017–2020: Its
   Aims and Means," in *Prosecuting Political Violence: Collaborative
   Research and Method*, ed. Michael Loadenthal (New York: Routledge,
   2021), 1–34.

7 At present, as of 20 September 2022, tPP has tracked and verified data on
   879 federal cases, as well as 80 cases brought by the City of Washington,
   DC. A data table tracking these cases has been made available to the general public, and was updated near daily throughout the weeks following
   the siege when prosecutions were announced.

8 This was years before I understood academic writing, and I cannot
   point to written artifacts beyond a host of inter-movement publications,
   typically authored through anonymous group monikers associated with
   Anti-Racist Action (ARA) or ad hoc formations.

9 For example, see: Michael Loadenthal, "Othering Terrorism: A Rhetorical
   Strategy of Strategic Labeling," in "Rethinking Genocide, Mass Atrocities,
   and Political Violence in Africa: New Directions, New Inquiries, and
   Global Perspectives," special issue, *Genocide Studies and Prevention: An
   International Journal* 13, no. 2 (June 2019): 74–105; Michael Loadenthal,
   "Asymmetric Labeling of Terrorist Violence as a Matter of Statecraft
   Propaganda: Or, Why the United States Does Not Feel the Need to Explain
   the Assassination of Osama Bin Laden," *Anarchist Developments in
   Cultural Studies* 0, no. 1 (2011): 113–39.

10 This includes at least fifteen publications; for example, see: Michael
   Loadenthal, "Nor Hostages, Assassinations, or Hijackings, but Sabotage,

Vandalism & Fire: 'Eco-Terrorism' as Political Violence Challenging the State and Capital," MLitt dissertation, St Andrews, Scotland, Centre for the Study of Terrorism and Political Violence, University of St Andrews, 2010; Michael Loadenthal, "Deconstructing 'Eco-Terrorism': Rhetoric, Framing and Statecraft as Seen through the Insight Approach," *Critical Studies on Terrorism* 6, no. 1 (April 2013), 92–117; Michael Loadenthal, "Eco-Terrorism? Countering Dominant Narratives of Securitisation: A Critical, Quantitative History of the Earth Liberation Front (1996–2009)," *Perspectives on Terrorism* (Center for Terrorism and Security Studies, Terrorism Research Initiative) 8, no. 3 (25 June 2014), 16–50; Michael Loadenthal, "'Eco-Terrorism': An Incident-Driven History of Attack (1973–2010)," *Journal for the Study of Radicalism* 11, no. 2 (fall 2017), 1–33; Michael Loadenthal and Lea Rekow, eds., *From Environmental Loss to Resistance: Infrastructure and the Struggle for Justice in North America* (Amherst: University of Massachusetts Press, 2020).

11 Emily Atkin, "A Database Showed Far-Right Terror on the Rise. Then Trump Defunded It," *The New Republic*, 3 January 2019, https://newrepublic.com/article/152675/database-showed-far-right-terror-rise-trump-defunded-it; Kristine Frazao, "Top Spot for Collecting Terrorism Data Defunded by the U.S. State Department," WJLA, 24 January 2019, https://wjla.com/news/nation-world/top-spot-for-collecting-terrorism-data-defunded-by-the-us-state-department.

12 Spencer Ackerman, "Research Indicates Trump Travel Ban Was Based on Misleading Data," *The Guardian*, 2 March 2017, http://www.theguardian.com/us-news/2017/mar/02/donald-trump-travel-ban-terrorism-data.

13 Alex Woodward, "'Fake News': A Guide to Trump's Favourite Phrase – and the Dangers It Obscures," *The Independent*, 2 October 2020, https://www.independent.co.uk/news/world/americas/us-election/trump-fake-news-counter-history-b732873.html.

14 Brett Samuels, "Trump Ramps Up Rhetoric on Media, Calls Press 'the Enemy of the People,'" *The Hill*, 5 April 2019, https://thehill.com/homenews/administration/437610-trump-calls-press-the-enemy-of-the-people.

15 Peter Beinart, "Trump Shut Programs to Counter Violent Extremism," *The Atlantic*, 29 October 2018, https://www.theatlantic.com/ideas/archive/2018/10/trump-shut-countering-violent-extremism-program/574237/; Eric Rosand, "International Efforts to Counter Violent Extremism under President Trump: A Case Study in Dysfunction and Incoherence," *Brookings*, 9 September 2020, https://www.brookings.edu/blog/order-from-chaos/2020/09/09/international-efforts-to-

counter-violent-extremism-under-president-trump-a-case-study-in-dysfunction-and-incoherence/.

16 Faiza Patel, Andrew Lindsay, and Sophia DenUyl, "Countering Violent Extremism in the Trump Era," *Brennan Center for Justice*, 15 June 2018, https://www.brennancenter.org/our-work/research-reports/countering-violent-extremism-trump-era.

17 Molly O'Toole, "Trump Officials Have Redirected Resources from Countering Far-Right, Racism-Fueled Domestic Terrorism," *Los Angeles Times*, 5 August 2019, https://www.latimes.com/politics/story/2019-08-05/trump-officials-have-redirected-resources-from-countering-far-right-racism-fueled-domestic-terrorism; Betsy Woodruff Swan, "They Tried to Get Trump to Care about Right-Wing Terrorism. He Ignored Them," POLITICO, 26 August 2020, https://www.politico.com/news/2020/08/26/trump-domestic-extemism-homeland-security-401926.

18 Salvador Rizzo, "President Trump's Claim That 'Nearly 3 in 4' Convicted of Terrorism Are Foreign-Born," *Washington Post*, 22 January 2018, https://www.washingtonpost.com/news/fact-checker/wp/2018/01/22/president-trumps-claim-that-nearly-3-in-4-convicted-of-terrorism-are-foreign-born/.

19 Sanya Mansoor, "Local Officials and Trump Were Quick to Blame Out-of-State Agitators for Minneapolis' Violent Protests. Arrest Records Suggest Otherwise," *Time*, 31 May 2020, https://time.com/5845680/out-of-state-agitators-minnesota-george-floyd-protests-barr/.

20 Donald Trump, "Remarks by President Trump in a Briefing on Wildfires, McClellan Park, CA," The White House, 14 September 2020, https://www.whitehouse.gov/briefings-statements/remarks-president-trump-briefing-wildfires-mcclellan-park-ca/.

21 Robert O. Paxton, "I've Hesitated to Call Donald Trump a Fascist. Until Now," *Newsweek*, 11 January 2021, https://www.newsweek.com/robert-paxton-trump-fascist-1560652.

22 Walter Laqueur, *Fascism: Past, Present, Future* (New York: Oxford University Press, 1996), 20–7; Robert O. Paxton, *The Anatomy of Fascism* (New York: Vintage, 2005), 139–40.

23 Hannah Arendt, *The Origins of Totalitarianism* (New York: Harvest, 1973), 305–91.

24 For example, see: Mary Louise Kelly and Mara Liasson, "Trump Refuses to Back Intelligence Agencies' Election Interference Findings," *All Things Considered*, 16 July 2018, NPR, https://www.npr.org/2018/07/16/629588424/trump-refused-to-say-he-believes-intelligence-agencies-election-interference-fin; Eileen Sullivan, "Trump Calls Intelligence

Officials 'Naive' After They Contradict Him," *New York Times*, 30 January 2019, https://www.nytimes.com/2019/01/30/us/politics/trump-intelligence.html.

25 Department of Justice, Office of Public Affairs, "Six Arrested on Federal Charge of Conspiracy to Kidnap the Governor of Michigan," *Department of Justice*, 8 October 2020, https://www.justice.gov/opa/pr/six-arrested-federal-charge-conspiracy-kidnap-governor-michigan.

26 Department of Justice, Office of Public Affairs, "Connecticut Man Charged with Attempting to Provide Material Support to ISIS," *Department of Justice*, 19 December 2019, https://www.justice.gov/opa/pr/connecticut-man-charged-attempting-provide-material-support-isis.

27 Department of Justice, Office of Public Affairs, "Twenty-Four Defendants, Including Alleged Aryan Circle Gang Members and Associates Indicted on Racketeering, Firearms, and Drug Charges in Multiple States," *Department of Justice*, 14 October 2021, https://www.justice.gov/opa/pr/twenty-four-defendants-including-alleged-aryan-circle-gang-members-and-associates-indicted.

28 As quoted in Dana Milbank, "In Trump's Mind, It's Always 'Really Sunny.' And That's Terrifying," *Washington Post*, 27 January 2017, https://www.washingtonpost.com/opinions/in-trumps-mind-its-always-really-sunny-and-thats-terrifying/2017/01/27/ff0a6278-e499-11e6-a547-5fb9411d332c_story.html.

29 Arendt, *Origins of Totalitarianism*, 397.

PART TWO

Outspoken Engagement

6

The Future of Design: Pursuing Spatial Justice and a Stronger Democracy

Thaïsa Way

What would landscape architecture, architecture, and planning look like if the primary metrics of success were what and how they contributed to spatial justice and to strengthening democracy in place? A privileging of justice and democracy would challenge a core concept that design is in any way neutral or innocent of broader cultural inscriptions for better or worse. It would demand an acknowledgment of the complicity of designers in the history of white supremacy and what Isabel Wilkerson describes as our American caste system.[1]

Designers are not without tools as they expand the practice of design as democracy and increase the importance of participatory design in practice and education.[2] It matters what is planned and designed, by whom, for whom, and what future it makes possible. Some designers are there already; others not so much. Students are demanding change that would re-imagine who designers are and what we do, and demanding that we return to the beginning, asking how we can measure success in ways that privilege spatial justice.

How would metrics of justice, equity, and democracy alter how and what we teach in design schools?[3] What is increasingly clear is that this work is not simple; it is not about tweaking the system or adding a seminar. It is about reckoning with the central role of ideas about whiteness, caste, and gender norms in design from its very earliest manifestations. It will require a radical revisioning of design as practice and as pedagogy. To centre spatial justice and democracy in design would demand the leadership of professionals simultaneously with a reconfiguration of the way we educate designers. Only then might we re-imagine design as a tool for moving toward spatial justice and in turn strengthening democracy.

The idea of neutrality is premised on the adage "Do no harm," an attitude embedded in the focus of the design professions on the "health, safety, and welfare" of the public. This is explicit in the profession's earliest definitions of practice from the late nineteenth and early twentieth centuries as architects aligned themselves with medicine and law. And this focus remains; as of 2022 the American Institute of Architects' statement still claims that the organization seeks "to advance our nation's quality of life and protect the public's health, safety and welfare." The American Society of Landscape Architects recognizes the leadership of designers in creating "healthy, beautiful, and resilient places for all." The American Planning Association is a bit more visionary in its claim to be responsible for "Creating Great Communities for All." In all these cases, the terms and metrics of success are left undefined. There is no reference to justice or equity as a core purpose of design, nor any recognition of the complicity of designers in creating the disparities, injustices, and violence of the built environment we know today. This absence suggests that we need to call for a re-evaluation of what it means to consider the health, safety, and welfare of communities or, more to the point, what makes a true and enduring "great community for all."

Acknowledging that design has agency and power requires that we describe what design does, whether its purpose is explicitly intended or "unintended," not only during the design process but in the *longue durée* of every project and community. It demands that we understand not only what design offers but to whom, for what reasons, and to what end. No project is an island. Such agency comes with responsibilities to the communities for which designs are created – as well as to the broader community. Designers have a responsibility to the future, to communities we can't yet know. This is daunting, and it should be.

Above all, acknowledging the agency and power of design demands that we write gender, race, identity, and difference back into design practice. This is not a new idea but one that recurs with each generation of designers as they struggle to position their practice in the wider world.[4] In 2004 George Lipsitz contended in his essay "The Racialization of Space and the Spacialization of Race" that "A primary goal of landscape architects and other citizens concerned with the built environment should be to disassemble the fatal links that connect race, place, and power."[5] More recently Richard H. Schein, in an essay titled "After Charlottesville," wrote that, despite all that has been done, we still need to "call out those moments in those landscapes; and engage and challenge the racial formations built on racist practice that the landscape is everywhere and always mediating."[6] And while there are individuals leading such work, as design professions writ large and as design schools, we remain woefully silent on this front beyond concerns about limited pipelines and excuses for a lack of diversity in our students, faculty, and leadership.

We are not without resources to do differently. Our strongest tools may well be in our design schools where we educate students and foster research and scholarship in and about design. To repeat, this is not about adding a class or refocusing a studio – or even hiring faculty of colour. It will be a messy reconfiguration of what it means to design and to teach design. It might begin by repositioning design from being solely a profession to being a way of thinking – not in the framework of design as iteration, but considering what it means to think about the world and life spatially and in place. So many disciplines have taken what they call a spatial turn, and yet designers – who base their work on spatiality – have rarely contributed in significant ways to these broader discussions. What knowledge might emerge if architects, planners, and landscape architects routinely partnered with sociologists, geographers, historians, and political scientists – not to mention ecologists, environmental scientists, public health researchers, and social workers – in research for the public good? Such partnerships would expand and enrich both research and teaching, bringing a much needed spatial literacy to the academy and, more important, to the public good. They would position design schools in intimate contact with the academy and the generation of knowledge.

The location of design schools within the academy is an asset that few – professionals, faculty, or, frankly, students – have taken full advantage of. Design schools are not autonomous entities but are deeply embedded in communities of scholars and teachers and learners of whom the vast majority are engaged in thinking about how to make a better world and what that might look like. Yes, design schools have reached out to the environmental sciences, engineering, and most recently to public health. These connections have been productive and the projects must continue. There is, however, a resource that even fewer have built upon, and that is the humanities.

A deeper engagement with the humanities is called for, now and in the future. The humanities, after all, are about humans, culture, and place; and questions of justice, equity, and democracy are fundamentally humanist questions. An inquiry engaged with the humanities might include study in philosophy and literature, to consider how cultures think and form belief systems about equity and community; in languages, to better understand how ideas of society and place are described and communicated; and in the disciplines of African-American, Indigenous, Latinx, and gender studies, for insights into socio-ecological relationships and frameworks.[7] A design education that engaged deeply with the humanities would strengthen the foundations for grappling with the complex and often-conflicting narratives present within any site, any community, and any project. Designers might then draw from important ideas and frameworks that have emerged from humanists explicitly seeking to better understand the human experience.

Concepts of intersectionality, as described by law professor Kimberlé Williams Crenshaw as well as by the work of the Combahee River Collective, could be critical to a more complex understanding of the overlapping dynamics of design, politics, culture, and ecology, among other forces that shape the built environment, physically and experientially.[8] Thinking in terms of intersectionality has been essential to the development of movements such as Black Lives Matter and Land Back. These movements shape space and take place. Designers should seek to understand such social and political movements and their potential. Cedric J. Robinson's description of racial capitalism offers the possibility of exploring how professions have been defined by their pursuit of profit and their distinction from those in the trades or labour forces.[9] Indigenous ways of knowing and reading land, community, and narrative are critical to understanding the role of design as a practice of settler colonialism. How, for instance, do we grapple with the complexities of designing stolen land? These are intellectual inquiries that demand to be at the centre of the design process if the measure of success is spatial justice and a stronger democracy that serves all.

Equally important is the need to understand the history of designers' and planners' complicity in oppression, white supremacy, and environmental degradation. History courses could be re-imagined to focus not on the lineage of self-defined professionals but rather on the built environment and communities in the context of a thick history of human interactions with place. Design schools might partner with faculty in history departments as well as with historians of science, medicine, and technology. These possibilities suggest that we need a "people's history of design"[10] that gives space to complex, messy, even conflicting narratives. It might engage diverse geographies as found in the work of Katherine McKittrick, Tiffany Lethabo King, and Max Liboiron, among others, who are curating counter-histories of everyday shaping of place and meaning in the land.[11] In one scenario, history courses might be integrated over the course of the professional education, building students' capacity to think like historians as they investigate questions about place and design inscriptions for our communities. Courses of this nature would in turn require historians to identify the tools needed for exploring how an accumulation and overlapping of identities might lead to unique manifestations of discrimination and privilege in the built environment. This knowledge would contribute to the design and planning of healthy communities for all.

Reformulating design pedagogy should also build on the critical growth of participatory design and community-engaged scholarship. Faculty working in design schools alongside practitioners – including Jeff Hou, Diane Jones Allen, Walter Hood, and David de la Peña – have developed critical approaches to rethinking the design process in ways that bring communities into discussions and foster alternative frameworks for imagining the role of the designer and design. Design as Democracy is an essential contribution to this work and should be deeply embedded in the curriculum, from seminars to studios. But designers cannot make change in a vacuum; community-engaged scholarship is equally essential. Such work is evident in the scholarship of Dr Andrea Roberts and the Texas Freedom Colonies Project, as communities collectively build a spatial atlas.[12] It is at the core of design scholarship by faculty such as Kofi Boone and Catherine Howett, as they develop community-based knowledge about place. It is apparent in the emergence of the Dark Matter University as a collaborative across design schools with the goal of rethinking the design studio, curated by planners, architects, landscape architects, and design historians including Justin Garrett Moore, Curry Hackett, Danielle Choi, Jelisa Blumberg, Jennifer Low, and Elgin Cleckley, among others.[13] There is momentum at this moment, but if designers and design schools don't take the reins we will lose the moment.

In the midst of COVID-19, Drs Dianne Harris and Cathy Davidson argued in an opinion essay in *Inside Higher Ed* that the pandemic offered an opportunity to rethink how we approach paedagogy, not at the scale of one faculty member or course, but at a leadership level: "What if college and university presidents saw this September not only as a campus emergency of epic proportions but also as an astonishing educational opportunity – a fall like no other, but in a good way? What if several announced, for example, that ... they would focus on something inspiring if necessarily general – say, community and care?"[14] Responding to the increasing visibility of extreme disparities in the pandemic's impact as well as the murder of yet another Black man by police, faculty from Columbia GSAPP issued "Unlearning Whiteness," a statement that called for an inter-rogation of the design school as a site of anti-Black racism that can only be understood "through a deep analysis and investigation of whiteness and white supremacy."[15] If we take these calls for action together, we can imagine redescribing design pedagogy, not by means of adding a new seminar or refocusing a studio course, but through a larger-scale overhaul of what it means to teach design and question to what end we construct design pedagogy.

Reconfiguring design pedagogy to centre on spatial justice in ways that foster a stronger democracy may well be the most significant contribution that design schools can make to their communities and to the broader role of design in building a better and more just future. The route will not be easy and certainly cannot be taken only on a school-by-school basis. Leadership will be needed to define design as spatial justice, to describe what design education might be. Schools will need to re-evaluate the role of accreditation standards and expectations of how they prepare students for professional engage-ment. New thinking may question who the students are and whether they wish to focus uniquely on a design profession or might be interested in learning to think spatially and through design in order to pursue careers in public service or international development, for example, or merely to be more informed citizens. A practical pos-sibility might be to move some skill building to professional offices or establishing flexible workshops in order to make time for students to learn across the academy. An approach such as this would validate the intellectual opportunities of the academy that are not readily available anywhere else – the capacity to pursue questions of humanity, justice, and democracy. None of this would be fast or straightforward. But if design schools don't change, neither will the professions. And if the professions don't change, designers will become increasingly irrelevant, both because they will continue to be complicit and because they will have no viable response to how do we can do better.

A further potential outcome that is worthy of consideration is the way in which such partnerships between design schools and the rest of the academy might change the university and higher education. Design school communities have rarely been acknowledged as critical contributors in research universities; and yet design thinking could be key to transforming higher education into a community of twenty-first-century institutions of the collective inquiry and knowledge that is needed for us to imagine a stronger democracy and a more equitable, just, and healthy future for all.

If we are to judge the success of design by its contributions to spatial justice and democracy, we must interrogate the capacity of the built environment to foster the growth of citizens' engagement with and trust in government, institutions, community, and – more to the point – power. This is what democracy is about. As noted by Danielle Allen and Eric Liu in the recent report "Our Common Purpose": "A healthy constitutional democracy depends on a virtuous cycle in which responsive political institutions foster a healthy civic culture of participation and responsibility, while a healthy civic culture – a combination of values, norms, and narratives – keeps our political institutions responsive and inclusive."[16] This cycle occurs in place. Design schools stand at the precipice of a new vision of the built environment as foundational to democracy, a vision that will in turn alter the academy where we teach designers. Design schools could lead not only the design and planning professions, but also the very idea of what it could mean to be educated as a citizen who understands and fosters spatial justice as the soul of a strong democracy.

NOTES

1 Isabelle Wilkerson, *Caste: The Origins of Our Discontents* (New York: Random House, 2020).

2 David de la Peña, Diane Jones Allen, Randolph T. Hester, Jeffrey Hou, Laura J. Lawson, and Marcia J. McNally, *Design as Democracy: Techniques for Collective Creativity* (Washington, DC: Island Press/Center for Resource Economics: Imprint: Island Press, 2017).

3 For the purposes of this argument, planning is viewed as an integral part of design in that its purpose is to envision and implement a future built environment in service of community.

4 Irene Cheng, Charles L. Davis, and Mabel O. Wilson, *Race and Modern Architecture: A Critical History from the Enlightenment to the Present* (Pittsburgh: University of Pittsburgh Press, 2020).

5 George Lipsitz, "The Racialization of Space and the Spatialization of Race: Theorizing the Hidden Architecture of Landscape," *Landscape Journal* 26, no. 1 (2007): 10–23.

6 Richard H. Schein, "After Charlottesville," *Southeastern Geographer* 58, no. 1 (2018): 12.

7 Resources include Chad Louis Williams, Kidada E. Williams, and Keisha N. Blain, *Charleston Syllabus: Readings on Race, Racism, and Racial Violence* (Athens: University of Georgia Press, 2016).

8 Devon W. Carbado, Kimberlé Williams Crenshaw, Vickie M. Mays, and Barbara Tomlinson, "INTERSECTIONALITY: Mapping the Movements of a Theory," *Du Bois Review* 10, no. 2 (2013): 303–12.

9 Cedric J. Robinson, H.L.T. Quan, and Ruth Wilson Gilmore, *Cedric J. Robinson: On Racial Capitalism, Black Internationalism, and Cultures of Resistance* (London: Pluto Press, 2019).

10 Howard Zinn, *A People's History of the United States: 1492–present* (20th anniversary ed.) (New York: HarperCollins, 1999).

11 Tiffany Lethabo King, *The Black Shoals: Offshore Formations of Black and Native Studies* (Durham: Duke University Press, 2019); Katherine McKittrick, *Demonic Grounds: Black Women and the Cartographies of Struggle* (Minneapolis: University of Minnesota Press, 2006); Max Liboiron, *Pollution Is Colonialism* (Durham: Duke University Press, 2021).

12 Texas Freedom Colonies, https://www.thetexasfreedomcoloniesproject.com/.

13 Dark Matter University, https://darkmatteruniversity.org/.

14 Cathy Davidson and Diane Harris, "Making Remote Learning Relevant," *Inside Higher Ed*, 5 August 2020, https://www.insidehighered.com/views/2020/08/05/colleges-should-throw-out-conventional-pedagogical-and-curricular-playbook-fall.

15 Amina Blacksher et al., *Unlearning Whiteness,* Black Faculty, GSAPP, Columbia University, 2020, https://unlearningwhiteness.cargo.site/.

16 Danielle Allen and Eric Liu, *Our Common Purpose: Reinventing American Democracy for the 21st Century* (Report to the American Academy of Arts & Sciences, 2020).

7

Activism as Arts Programming

Amelia Jones

The world as privileged Euro-Americans imagined it from the Enlightenment through the change of the millennium (with a few savage bumps such as First and Second World Wars along the way) has come to an end. What seemed like a fairly brisk decay of the sanctity of European values, starting at least with the Great War, has accelerated rapidly with the events of the twenty-first century – from 9/11 to the rise of nationalisms across the Western world, to the economic crashes of 2008 and 2020, to the exposure of the hypocrisy of Euro-American concepts of equality and freedom with the increasingly persistent public and visual evidence of violence against Black and brown and Asian bodies in the Euro-American context since the mid-twentieth century. With each catastrophe has come a wave of neoliberal ideology bent on papering over a collapsing system. Art has played a huge role in that papering over.

Here, via one potent case study, I propose strategies to counter the covert toxicity of what I call the "global" (in scare quotes, for reasons that will become obvious) art complex, and look at responses to the structural racism and violence in our worlds, which the "global" art complex arguably perpetuates. I explore how and why it is that performance and/or performative curatorial practices – which are effectively activist modes of addressing oppression and violence while opening the gallery system to new communities – are pivotal critical responses to the failures of this art complex to support and nurture.

"Curate," of course, as many curatorial studies scholars have pointed out, is derived from the Latin *cura*, which means "to care" (the original curators in Europe were caring for arrays of objects in cabinets of curiosity and other personal collections, before the development of municipal or national art and natural history museums).

Far from existing as an inherently caring profession, however, curatorial work over the past decades, even when well intended, has most often aided and abetted the forces of the so-called global art complex. Under the guise of being global, glamorous international art fairs and events are peddled. And yet they are most often sponsored either by dictatorial governments that seek to gloss over their violence and reactionism or by private corporations that monetize art while simultaneously touting its supposedly ethereal and transcendent values. And the art that they present is almost always produced by people identifying as artists in the Euro-American sense, trained usually in Euro-American art schools. How global is this kind of so-called art (itself an English word, a European conceit)? We can see the exposed structures of the supposedly global art complex very clearly now that it has been stopped overnight by quarantines and the termination of international air travel.

Most curators signed up to produce global exhibitions are forced to participate (or don't realize they are participating) fully in the global commodification of world visual culture – the neoliberal joining of disparate works from around the world as art, contributing to the burgeoning of tourism – through an entirely European system and Euro-American standards and values. Art is not incidental to the success of Europe's violent subjugation of colonized and enslaved peoples. And this constructed system of values in relation to art has had concrete effects. From the beginning it was built into European education, architecture, all forms of culture, and the fabric of burgeoning early modern and modern urban centres in and beyond Europe. Following this logic, European cities founded art museums in the late eighteenth and nineteenth centuries to house objects hallowed as works of art. During the same period they established museums of natural history to contain and display objects considered to be artifacts. The spaces Europeans and American citizens inhabit are literally divided from those of the colonized according to this hierarchical logic.

Activist methods in curatorial work, I assert, are key to counteracting this passive reinforcement of neoliberal late-capitalist structures of power in the so-called global art context. Activist art is a more limited concept, given that, to be effective in promoting change in the social, political, or economic realm, discrete works of art are (to say the least) ineffectual. Activism as arts programming is a broader and more appropriately performative concept that encompasses some of the most vital work that artists are pursuing in the public sphere today – broadening the effect of art that can be mobilized to connect to communities beyond the usual "global" art audiences. In the current chaotic and violent moment of late-stage capitalism, emerging artists who are politically ambitious are increasingly motivated toward creative political organizing rather than, strictly speaking, making things. Art is increasingly evanescent and engaged – a set of actions that can be curatorial – rather than oriented toward a specific marketplace.

This brief essay will explore a key example of such strategic modes of activist programming from Los Angeles around 2020 – the South Central neighbourhood arts centre of Crenshaw Dairy Mart (CDM), co-founded by Patrisse Cullors (one of the original founders of Black Lives Matter), noé olivas, and Alexandre Dorriz; the centre's name is based on its home location in a building with this name from a defunct dairy mart. CDM integrates performance programming with exhibitions on histories of activism and work engendered through their own activism, and connects community discussions and voting drives through close collaboration with local artists, musicians, and other creatives, answering the call for art to enact rather than depict, to perform rather than narrate.

For the sake of transparency, I note here that all three of the founders – Cullors, Dorriz, and olivas – were students of mine in the University of Southern California Roski School of Art and Design MFA department, graduating in 2018. As well, Cullors, as noted above, is internationally known for having co-founded Black Lives Matter (with Alicia Garza and Opal – now Ayọ – Tometi) in 2013 after the vigilante murder of Trayvon Martin and the acquittal of his murderer in Florida. Both of these facts are important in understanding the approach of CDM.

As stated on its website, CDM's mission is at the same time utopian and pragmatic:

JUST SOUTH OF MANCHESTER AND OFF OF CRENSHAW
STANDS TALL A FORMER DAIRY MART, HOME TO AN
ARTIST COLLECTIVE AND ART GALLERY DEDICATED
TO SHIFTING THE TRAUMA-INDUCED CONDITIONS
OF POVERTY AND ECONOMIC INJUSTICE, BRIDGING
CULTURAL WORK AND ADVOCACY, AND INVESTIGATING
ANCESTRIES THROUGH THE LENS OF INGLEWOOD
AND ITS COMMUNITY.

WHAT THESE BLACK AND TRANSNATIONAL
IDENTITIES SEEK IS AN IMAGINATION OF NEW COLLEC-
TIVE MEMORY THROUGH PROGRAMMING, EVENTS, AND
ARTS INSTALLATIONS WHICH CULTIVATE AND NURTURE
COMMUNAL ARTS AND EDUCATION.
     THE CRENSHAW DAIRY MART EMERGES FROM AN
INVESTMENT IN ABOLITION, MODES OF ACCESSIBILITY
IN ART PRACTICE, AND WEAVING COMMUNITY SOLI-
DARITY THROUGH NEW MEMORIES.[1]

The collective asserts its primary concern with curation and art-
making and performing as inexorably linked to healing and care on
its opening web page, as well as through its most visible public project
to date. "Care Not Cages," drawing on Cullors's years-long work
fighting against the mass incarceration of African Americans, aims to
"GENERATE LESS CONTACT WITH POLICE, LESS INCARCERA-
TION, LESS CAGING, LESS TRAUMA AND MORE HEALING."[2]
This project, in their words, is driven by a denunciation of "racial
capitalism and our government's addiction to greed, punishment, and
man-made disaster," and an acknowledgment that "black, poor, disabled, trans and queer [communities] and communities at the margins
will be impacted the most" by COVID-19.[3] The group raised funds
in order to run a competition among incarcerated people to produce
artworks on the theme of "Care Not Cages," awarding three artists
the top prizes, as well as granting an additional eight smaller awards.
All awards included funds payable either to the artist or (if still incarcerated) to their families.

This particular Care Not Cages initiative seeks to empower those
oppressed by incarceration specifically by valuing and encouraging
their creative work. CDM is an example of a political, artistic, and
social initiative that merges activism quite directly with community
work and visual arts production. While on a completely different scale
from large international curatorial initiatives – such as, for example,
Nigerian curator Okwui Enwezor's Documenta11 (a bold and decolonizing effort to move this major art event to multiple sites of
conversation or "platforms" around the world, including New Delhi,
Lagos, and St Lucia) – the CDM collective labours on a local level to
make art *work*.[4] Its curators put art to work against the grain of what
Enwezor called "Westernism" – a term he coined to encapsulate "that
sphere of global totality that manifests itself through the political,

social, economic, cultural, juridical, and spiritual integration achieved via institutions devised and maintained solely to perpetuate the influence of European and North American modes of being," asserting itself as "the only viable idea of social, political, and cultural legitimacy from which modern subjectivities are seen to emerge."[5]

This art "working" via CDM is itself performative, striving primarily to activate and give agency to communities and to produce social change. As mentioned, the artist-activists Dorriz, Cullors, and olivos all attended a highly organized twenty-first-century MFA program at my own institution, USC Roski (one could argue that Roski is an art-school analogue of the global art exhibition, given the corporate nature of USC, which is a private university). However, in the classroom at Roski – where our core courses include students both from our MA Curatorial Practices and our MFA Art programs – we focus on decolonial approaches as well as thinking across art-making and curating, with an emphasis on interfaces with the public sphere. The participation of Dorriz, Cullors, and olivas in these classes exemplified the way in which our students tend to push back and reciprocally to inform what we do moving forward as an institution. CDM is a thrilling example of a potential public manifestation or outcome of what we hope to be a decolonizing and empowering curriculum, one that pivots around questions rather than asserting methods or channelling student energies along time-worn paths.

Enwezor worked on a macro level, pushing beyond the traditional Kassel (Germany) site of Documenta by expanding it to international, non-European platforms beyond what he spoke of as the Euro-centric art world with its "tendentious claims of radicality."[6] For Enwezor, however, bold curatorial initiatives and individual artworks must work together, one on a macro level, the other on a micro level attuned to individual viewers. In the catalogue to Documenta 11, on the micro level, he thus asserted that the structures of spectatorship are foundational elements to consider in relation to any aspirations of shifting the so-called global art world's entrenched systems of value and power. In the catalogue he wrote that the exhibition and its platforms were meant to acknowledge spectatorship as "central and fundamental to all forms of valuation of the visual content of an exhibition," and asserted: "Spectatorship can only function productively in a democratic, open system ... In the democratic system ... *one that promotes agency over pure belief*, the demands of citizenship place strong ethical constraints on the artist based on his or her commitment to all 'forms-of-life.' The practice of art presents the artist with the task of making such a commitment."[7]

In this way, no art discourse or institution can move forward in a way consonant with progressive ideals (that is, as liberal art institutions claim to aspire to) without working on both levels to push for change. CDM both establishes a radically welcoming site for neighbourhood community expansion (within the remit of art, loosely speaking) and works with individuals (such as the incarcerated or formerly incarcerated with the Care Not Cages initiative). Like Documenta 11, it is also fundamentally driven by the energies of those formerly excluded from the "global" (but really Euro-American–centric) art world (Enwezor was from Nigeria; Dorriz's family is Iranian American; Cullors's family is African American; olivas's family is Latinx). As per Enwezor's strategies, those working to produce structural change successfully must infiltrate all levels – micro and macro – of cultural institutions to put culture in motion (here, for example, the CDM parties, documented on Cullors's hugely successful Instagram account, contribute to CDM's more institutional work). In contrast to the reactionary liberalism of the tick-box or multicultural approaches of the global art complex, this strategy of infiltration asserts voices that demand structural change. In order to hear these voices and incorporate them, institutions must change on both micro and macro levels. This means making and curating art differently, perhaps even dropping the idea of art as it has existed to date in the still–Euro-American, anglophone, and white dominant structures of the not-so-global art complex.

NOTES

This paper is taken from a much longer analysis in Amelia Jones, "Ethnic Envy and Other Aggressions in the Contemporary 'Global' Art Complex," NKA: *Journal of Contemporary African Art*, Special Issue: "Okwui Enwezor: The Art of Curating," edited by Jane Chin Davidson and Alpesh Patel, no. 48 (2021): 96–110.

1 See https://www.crenshawdairymart.com/about-us; accessed 21 March 2021.
2 Ibid.
3 See https://www.crenshawdairymart.com/care-not-cages; accessed 21 March 2021.

4 For a full description of Enwezor's 2002 Documenta11, see my "Ethnic Envy and Other Aggressions in the Contemporary 'Global' Art Complex."

5 Okwui Enwezor, "The Black Box," *Documenta 11_Platform 5: Exhibition* (Kassel: Documenta; and Ostfildern-Ruit: Hatje Cantz Publishers, 2002), 45–6.

6 Ibid.

7 Ibid, 54; Enwezor was citing Giorgio Agamben on "forms-of-life," from Giorgio Agamben, *Means without End: Notes on Politics*, trans. Vincenzo Binetti and Cesare Casarino (Minneapolis: University of Minnesota Press, 2000), 3–4.

Space for Black Joy

Cleo Davis and Kayin Talton

Space is a necessity of life. Space to celebrate, mourn, grow, breathe, and refresh. To live. To matter. Black Americans have long had to carve out space for these life needs out of places not specifically designed for them. And too often, once these niches have become neighbourhoods and communities, they are destroyed under the guise of urban renewal. This has occurred in numerous Black communities across the nation.

One might say the practice of creating space for life's purposes falls into the category of "urbanist" – our combined knowledge and experience in multidisciplinary areas of art, design, engineering, urban planning, cultural-historic preservation, and research bring a unique and productive variety to our areas of practice and knowledge. However, "urbanist" does not fully exemplify the intent within our creative endeavours; nor does it fully express the impact that we are striving for within the Black community and in the City of Portland as a whole. We consider ourselves to be "social construct artists," utilizing both creative and administrative processes to create change in both the built and social environment. This term more clearly exemplifies the depth and impact that we aim to put into our practice. As social construct artists we have integrated disciplines and ideas to have an impact on the built and social environment within the City of Portland for Black residents, and created reBuilding Cornerstones, a studio and practice focused on such changes in design fields.

A HISTORY OF EXCLUSION

This essay focuses on the need to address current issues and problems by honestly reviewing the past – a past full of and built upon designed inequities that cannot be defended in 2021.

On the local level, when Oregon was not yet a territory, there were those who claimed the land inhabited by Indigenous people as a "White Utopia." Laws prohibiting slavery (1843) and then banning all free Black people (1844) were approved as part of the original Oregon constitution. Over the next several years, exclusion laws were revised from mandating public whipping of up to thirty-nine lashes for Black people who remained within the state for more than six months, to requiring forced labour for those found in the state after sundown. Though voted down in 1845, that law was replaced in 1849 by a law of the Oregon Territorial Legislature forbidding any "negro or mulatto to enter into or reside within the limits of this Territory." Land donation and the Homestead Act followed, creating opportunities for white colonists and those with a specified mix of "Indian" blood to own land. With the exclusion laws still in effect, sundown towns a reality, and a $5 tax enacted in 1862 targeting Black, Chinese, and Indigenous Hawaiian people, Black people were denied the right to stay in Oregon by law until 1926. Such laws and racist language were not fully removed from the Oregon constitution until 2000.

Despite the exclusion laws, the number of Black people in Oregon continued to grow. Much of the burgeoning late-nineteenth-century Black community in Portland was centred in the northwest area of the city around the train station. Black-owned businesses like the Golden West Hotel and the Chandler & Bessilien Club Cafe, among others, supported the growing community. With the 1913 opening of the Broadway Bridge connecting northwest Portland to Albina, the community began to expand. The growing number of Black residents did not go unnoticed. Shortly thereafter, in 1919, the Portland Board of Realty approved a "Code of Ethics" prohibiting realtors and bankers from selling property in white neighbourhoods to people of colour or providing mortgages for such purchases, thereby reinforcing the impact of previous exclusion laws.[1]

Lower Albina became Portland's largest Black urban enclave, shaped by two major events: labour migration during the Second World War, and the 1948 flooding of Vanport City, the largest single wartime development in the United States and Oregon's second-largest city.[2]

Vanport, Oregon, was formed by Henry Kaiser as workers from across the nation poured into the area to work in the Kaiser shipyards, built to sustain war efforts. The newly formed Housing Authority of Portland was less than accommodating to the newcomers. Although sometimes viewed as an exercise in diversity, it still suffered from systemic racist practices. Housing for Black residents was built more cheaply than homes for their white counterparts, and job offerings were just as prejudiced. Nearby, white Portlanders were concerned about the "New Negro Migrants."[3] "White Trade Only" signs were common, as were reminders of the presence of the Ku Klux Klan. After the war ended, many newcomers either returned to their places of origin, or moved on to other areas. However, this did not happen quickly or completely enough for many white Oregonians.

The Memorial Day flood of 1948 came as no real surprise; the Columbia River was noticeably high and had overflowed its banks further upstream. However, only days before, the Housing Authority of Portland had reassured the remaining residents of Vanport that they were safe. Ruby Lee Talton, visiting family in Vanport that day, recalled it being a beautiful, sunny day when they suddenly heard what they thought was an explosion: it was the levees failing. The water poured in rapidly and many were left with just minutes to reach safety.

Albina was the only area in Portland where former Black residents of Vanport could go. Restrictive covenants and redlining were well established, the latter specifically restricting access to homeownership and loans.[4] That same year, Oregon realtors adopted the "National Realtors Code" (based on an earlier state law), which proclaimed that "a realtor shall never introduce into a neighborhood members of any race or nationality whose presence will be detrimental to property values."

Though practised well into the 1990s, redlining and other property restrictions have only recently been a subject of more public research and discussion, even with the lived experiences of Black people widely voiced and documented.

POLICIES AND PROCESSES OF DESTRUCTION AND DISINVESTMENT

During our artist residency at the City of Portland Archives and Records Center (PARC), which began in 2018, we researched current and past policies resulting in the disinvestment of communities and neighbourhoods, Black communities in particular. In our research, we were able to find documentation substantiating personal family history with red-tagging, blight removal, and nuisance ordinances – documentation we then used to shine a light on long-overlooked racist policies and practices.

In ways just as insidious as the racist covenants lurking within the deeds of Portland's older homes, zoning patterns have created a legacy of exclusion and fuelled speculation and displacement. Once a city of single "residential" zones, where housing of many types coexisted in the same neighbourhood, Portland has been intentionally segregated through the creation of a series of single-dwelling zones, where only one house is allowed on a lot. Furthermore, community plans in areas with larger populations of people of colour received more multi-family zoning plans, while areas with larger white populations preserved a high proportion of single-dwelling zones.

The term "blight" kick-started the erasure of Black prosperity from the 1940s through to the 1990s, with the city seizing numerous Black-owned homes or targeting them with fines and intimidation, forcing many families to move – all under the guise of "slum clearance" and "urban renewal." Blight was a term used fairly synonymously with predominantly Black and other "undesirable" neighbourhoods. According to an official document from the Portland Bureau of Buildings from 1962, blight included roof leaks, loose steps, doors that "stick," uncovered trash, and even seemingly ambiguous charges such as "needs paint" and "needs clean up." Some homes were even targeted for having "outdated" items like now highly coveted clawfoot tubs.

"Red-tagging" is a term frequently used by municipal building departments to describe the posting of notices on a property deemed dangerous or uninhabitable by a county or city. Officially, this means that the property has a recorded lien or liens against it due to code enforcement violations. The fact that a structure has been red-tagged does not necessarily mean that it must be condemned; but it is an official warning that remediation is required. Red-tagging was used liberally in Black communities, and leveraged as a tool to remove wealth and stability from Black families and businesses.

The approval of the construction of the Memorial Coliseum in 1956 brought more destruction to the still reeling community. To make way for the development, 476 homes were razed, as were commercial buildings. That same year, federal funds became available through the Federal-Aid Highway Act, for the purpose of creating more streamlined transportation systems for suburban residents on what would be Interstate 5 and Highway 99. Again, the path was cleared through Albina, demolishing hundreds of housing units and cutting a gash through the neighbourhood and community.

CREEPY IS RIGHT FOLKS!

He can do what he says — IF YOU
LET HIM. He's been doing it in Portland
for years. Wherever you live in the city,
you don't have to travel very far for
visible proof.

WHAT TO DO?

The Conservation Rehabilitation Program of the Portland Bureau of Buildings
is undoing much of Creepy's past work
with its ordinances and Housing and
Neighborhood Improvement Program.
BUT THIS IS NOT ENOUGH —

YOU MUST HELP!

You can help by carefully inspecting
your property for signs of Creepy Blight
and getting rid of him with paint, repairs
or modernization wherever it is necessary.

Your property is probably the largest
single investment you have ever made.
Don't risk it by letting it fall into a state
of disrepair.

FOR FURTHER INFORMATION
Contact
Conservation Rehabilitation
PORTLAND
BUREAU OF BUILDINGS
Room 403 • City Hall • Portland
CApitol 8-6141, Ext. 437

Figure 8.1 1962 Creepy Blight flyer.

The building of the I-5 highway in the middle of Portland's Black
neighbourhood not only destroyed a vibrant community but has also
had a long-lasting environmental and social impact. The exhaust
fumes from the highway and traffic at bridges, the heat generated
from asphalt and concrete pavement, and the removal of land from
community use are examples of environmental and economic injustices that need to be acknowledged and repaired so that the city and
nation can heal.

Figure 8.2 Aerial view of the path of Highway I-5 through Albina after razing.

Figure 8.3a 1950s. High aerial view of Inner N Portland.

Figure 8.3b 2021. Aerial view of Inner N Portland.

Figure 8.3c 1948. Aerial view of the Vanport Flood Broadway Bridge (Inner Albina) during Vanport flood.

Figure 8.3d 2021. Aerial view of Inner Albina.

With the loss of so much housing within the community, displaced residents were pushed further north and east, often into the older homes within the surrounding areas. Because of red-lining, loans and financing for larger repairs were not available. Combining this with the Housing Act of 1957, local officials continued targeting the Black community, deeming their neighbourhood "blighted" and labelling it as "slums" in need of revitalization.[5]

The organizations, agencies, and developments may have had different names and faces across the nation, but the goal and effect was the same – the destruction of Black communities for the convenience and wealth of white entities and communities.

LIFTING UP BLACK VOICES

With the advent of the worldwide COVID-19 pandemic in 2020, business as usual was interrupted and in some cases completely shut down. Access to technology – or the lack thereof – highlighted the disparities of policing, healthcare, and governing systems. Though the specific Black Lives Matter movement coalesced in 2013 with the acquittal of George Zimmerman in the killing of Trayvon Martin, a seventeen-year-old Black youth, the highly televised and streamed 2020 murder of George Floyd by police officer Derek Chauvin was the match that ignited the powder keg. Demonstrations erupted internationally, bringing even more attention to long-simmering issues.

As a result, local organizations, cities, and government entities began to look for ways to recognize demands for change. Streets were painted overnight, statues and monuments honouring those who had abused Black people and fought to keep them enslaved were ripped from their bases, and murals calling for justice sprang up on boarded windows. This was the people's art, creating a more just environment in which it is clear that Black lives do matter.

This *ad hoc* redesign of the built environment reflects how often the input and the experience of marginalized communities, even as the primary denizens, are overlooked or ignored. Moving forward without engaging people who are affected but excluded from involvement in the needed changes will not work: the current problem-solving process is not acceptable. A Eurocentric paradigm cannot be used to serve all people. Those who are economically "rich" and have the decision-making power cannot treat human beings like "objects" that must be pushed away, ignored, marginalized, jailed, or controlled.[6]

The patterns of restriction and exclusion of Black communities from opportunities for wealth-building are quite evident. Change cannot truly be effected until this and similar facts are addressed. Future models for facing issues and solving problems that Black people experience must focus on developing ideas, strategies, and plans that acknowledge the impact and harm that have been inflicted on Black people. Such models will need to:

- identify root causes – including ideals of white supremacy –
  and tackle them with facts, truth, and integrity. People may say
  they had no role in creating past problems; however, they have
  benefited from the systems designed in their favour;
- develop a new paradigm with the authentic voices of those who
  have been harmed or affected by previous decisions;
- consistently engage methods and/or models that ensure that
  decisions are implemented so as to avoid repeating previous
  mistakes or creating new mistakes or issues;
- focus on policing, the criminal justice system, repaying education
  debt, spatial justice, economic stability, and making reparations
  to those who have never been able to get out of harm's way
  because of unjust systems of oppression.

Figure 8.4 Sky Block concept.

Figure 8.5 Sky Block interior spaces.

ALBINA VISION TRUST

The Albina Vision Trust in Portland has investigated such goals as it moves forward with planning a new future for Albina – a future in which its Black inhabitants thrive in community, create and maintain generational wealth, and benefit from the area's development. An Albina in which the street grid is restored and reconnected. A space of Black joy.

Governance as a tool of community maintenance and wealth generation is one of the tenets of this project as well. Some of the constructive possibilities are that:

- loans and funds be processed through Black-owned banks;
- Global Majority–owned firms be prioritized in awarding contractor bids – with local firms given first priority;
- local residents – particularly those who have been displaced – be given priority for employment on projects;
- protection from Eminent Domain regulations and policies be written into policy;
- policing be community based;
- a legacy of art, architecture, and business be brought in and restored.

THE SKY BLOCK CONCEPT

A more conceptual approach is presented here, as the "Sky Block," a concept we developed in partnership with El Dorado design firm. The focus here is on the use of architectural methods to address the economic, social, and cultural norms that are core to Black Americans' dispersed communities as they are given the right to return to the city centre of Portland, Oregon. Rather than expect Black people who were displaced by urban renewal to return to high-rise condominiums and small apartments that lack green spaces, gardens, front porches, and common ground where friends and neighbours can gather and enjoy themselves, Sky Block introduces a social and physical infrastructure that elevates and stacks entire neighbourhood blocks. This innovation creates an environment where intact communities can be created and cultural norms can be continued within a skyscraper typology. Placing the structure over a capped freeway creates numerous implications in the realm of environmental justice: reduction of emissions through the provision of filtration; cooling of the "heat island effect" from the concrete and asphalt, thanks to an increase in green spaces; and lessening of the noise pollution generated by the highway.

CONCLUSION

Black Portlanders have consistently been denied both space and a voice in the decision-making about the places they inhabit, an experience that is replicated across the nation. This cannot continue to happen. Instead, a design culture of inclusion of the voice and desires of the very communities we work with must become the norm. Lift up Black voices, and partner in cultivating spaces of Black joy!

NOTES

1 Elaine Rector, "Looking Back in Order to Move Forward: An Often Untold History Affecting Oregon's Past, Present and Future Timeline of Oregon and U.S. Racial, Immigration and Education History," *Coaching for Educational Equity*, 2010, https://www.portlandoregon.gov/civic/article/516558.

2 Karen J. Gibson, "Bleeding Albina: A History of Community Disinvestment, 1940–2000," *Transforming Anthropology* 15, no. 1 (2007): 3–25.

3 "New Negro Migrants Worry City," *The Oregonian*, Portland, Oregon, 29 September 1942.

4 Jena Hughes et al., "Historical Context of Racist Planning: A History of How Planning Segregated Portland," *Portland Bureau of Planning and Sustainability,* September 2019, https://www.portland.gov/sites/default/files/2019-12/portlandracistplanninghistoryreport.pdf.

5 Gibson, "Bleeding Albina," 3–25.

6 Edwin J. Nichols, *The Philosophical Aspects of Cultural Difference* (Washington, DC: Nichols and Associates, 1974, 1987, 2004).

9

Hegel and Netflix

Alex Taek-Gwang Lee

"MY BOSS IS NOT HUMAN"

The COVID-19 pandemic does not in itself constitute a crisis of capitalism; rather, it compounds existing problems within the capitalist mode of production. The precarious status of essential workers, regardless of their living condition, has worsened. By contrast, as a result of valorizing the market above all else, unrestricted capitalist accumulation has been more efficient and has exacerbated social inequality. These contradictory consequences of the pandemic situation prove that capitalism does not need workers for its completion. The pandemic has served less as a moment to mark the end of capitalism than as yet another moment to sustain its paradox.

Indeed, what we are seeing at the moment are the more traumatic experiences of capitalist restructuring. Some critics use the concept of "shock doctrine" to explain how capitalism survives the process of disasters. Naomi Klein's theory of the shock doctrine, her critique of the Chicago School, is based on the assumption that "the human cost of shock therapy" is tactically designed to control the working class.[1] The foundation of shock doctrine is undoubtedly the human behavioural realm and it essentially requires a disruption in the social relations of production. However, given its current prevalence, disaster capitalism seems to achieve its culmination by erasing the working class itself. By that I do not mean the removal of workers but the modification of work as such.

In the current pandemic this modification dramatically evolves to the idea of mechanical management based on surveillance technology. In other words, the mechanization of work – a perversion of

Taylorism – reconstructs the fundamentals of the labour force and drives each worker to be a part of a mechanism. The financial bull market on technology investment precipitates this shift further and reformulates the distribution of labour. I would call this inversion of capitalism the very essence of "pure capitalism"; that is, the "free" economic system that encourages individuals' voluntary competition to produce and trade without government intervention. It is not easy to determine where administrative interference can engage the system if workers have no human management. "My Boss Is Not Human" (我的領导不是人), an article recently published in *Caijing*, a Chinese economic magazine, demonstrates how such mechanical surveillance can reorganize the workplace.[2]

According to the report, many Chinese enterprises have adopted artificial intelligence for more efficient and standardized management. The new system works with surveillance cameras positioned throughout workplaces and records every worker's behaviour and activities. An electronic roll call at the entrance is necessary to identify each person and monitor the group. This algorithmic scrutiny, the mechanical transformation of all human actions into data, subsumes the whole process of work into that of a single machine. The monitoring camera transcribes workers' performance per second, and the central operating system verifies its efficiency. Each component is designated a prescribed processing time by the algorithm, and the "Intelligent Task Distribution System" will recognize and facilitate the prescribed sequences of the workers' actions. The electronic time attendance system refines the check-in procedures previously set at the company gate. Workers must swipe their cards if they leave the workplace. If they are absent from their seats for more than fifteen minutes, that recorded data will be submitted to the central operating system, and the corresponding wages will be automatically deducted at the end of the month.

My point concerning this Chinese version of Taylor's scientific management does not lie in the fact that Orwell's imagination of Big Brother has been realized but rather in the fact that the aim of the administration is to modify human behaviour for the sake of the algorithmic mechanism. There is no such thing as Big Brother in the system; there is only the technological stupidity of controlling the workers by simplifying their actions. Any digressive and unpredicted move does not seem to be allowed. However, workers follow the rules not because the system governs them so tightly but because the norm of the new scientific management – that is, the command of mechanical surveillance – forces them to obey the axioms of the mechanism. Therefore, the algorithmic organization of the workplace is not a crucial factor in the new management. The problem is that there must be an invisible decision-maker behind the automatic system that can solve any accidental and unpredictable outcome, even though the algorithmic mechanism operates without the presence of the human boss in the venue. The absence of surveillance – that is, subjective articulation – is always already included in the mechanism and preserves the locus of resistance. My experience of Netflix during this pandemic would suggest an example to justify this assumption.

ALGORITHM AND CHOICE

Recently I watched two films: Bollywood's *Love Per Square Foot* (2018) and Hollywood's *Leap Year* (2010). I discovered contrasting messages in these different productions. *Love Per Square Foot* portrays wish-fulfillment in the young Indian middle class, while *Leap Year* presents American middle-class disillusionment. The Indian movie is about an Indian boy (Sanjay, an IT engineer) and an Indian girl (Karina, a cashier) who work in the same bank. They both have dreams of owning their own "house" but are constantly deflected by their personal lives. Sanjay has an affair with his boss, who refuses to leave her husband, while Karina becomes engaged to her boyfriend, but her mother dithers about her dream of owning a house. Everything starts to change, however, when Sanjay finds out about a "joint housing scheme" that is supposed to provide an available apartment to a newly married couple. He suggests that he and Karina apply for it together, and she agrees to his plan to lie to the authorities that they are married.

Leap Year follows the journey of Anna Brady, a real estate worker who is heading to Dublin to propose to Jeremy, her boyfriend, on leap day. (On 29 February, according to Irish tradition, a man cannot reject a woman's proposal for marriage.) Anna and Jeremy live in Boston together, but he has not yet proposed. His hesitation is the impetus for her decision to embark on her leap-year adventure. On the way to Dublin, she meets an Irishman, Declan, an innkeeper and chef. No public transportation being available on her arrival, she begs Declan to taxi her to Jeremy's hotel. In typical romantic-comedy fashion, of course, they gradually discover a mysterious attachment to each other.

After many twists and turns, they finally reach the hotel, where Jeremy – surprisingly – proposes to Anna. His intention does not fulfil Anna's dream, however. At their later engagement party in Boston, she learns that he proposed only because the co-op board of the apartment building they want to buy in has an unspoken rule that only married couples can move in together. Disappointed, Anna leaves Jeremy and goes back to Ireland to confirm her true love, Declan.

Interestingly, these two films deal with marriage and housing, the material foundations of the middle class, but in quite contrasting ways. For the Indian couple, housing is the necessary fulfilment to their love but, for the American heroine, prioritizing property indicates fake love, which she decides to renounce for true love. I happened to discover them on Netflix: *Love Per Square Foot* first and then *Leap Year*. I didn't "intend" to watch two movies one after another. It was Netflix that led me to *Leap Year* after I had watched *Love Per Square Foot*.

This recommendation would have been programmed into Netflix's algorithm. In other words, my taste in movie selections is read by the new teleo-technology of mechanical categorization. Without this technology, I could not have watched two films consecutively, let alone reach a comparative understanding of them. My contingent experiences of two movies took place via artificial intelligence. Without a doubt, it was "me" who chose the second movie and decided to watch it after checking Netflix's recommendations, but it was not "my purpose" that brought me to the choice and decision. Even my hesitation about taking just a few of moments for my pleasure does not belong to the machine. The logic of Netflix relies heavily on my arbitrary choices. That feeling of reluctance makes us believe that "we can choose" or "we have a will to select."

TELEOLOGY VS MECHANISM

Netflix is a mechanism that seems to have no purpose determined by an intelligence external to itself. Even though it is called artificial intelligence, Netflix does not have intelligence; but it confuses us with deferred moments of choice and functions as if we had a purpose in picking out something. It is a mere mechanism that assembles random big data and makes them seem necessitated. Half in jest, Hegel already anticipated the advent of Netflix in his discussion of the distinction between mechanism and teleology. In *The Science of Logic*, he argued that "where there is the perception of a *purposiveness*, an *intelligence* is assumed as its author; required for purpose is thus the concept's own free concrete existence." He continues:

> *Teleology* is above all contrasted with *mechanism*, in which the determinateness posited in the object, being external, is one that gives no sign of *self-determination*. The opposition between *causæ efficientes* and *causæ finales*, between merely *efficient* and *final causes*, refers to this distinction, just as, at a more concrete level, the enquiry whether the absolute essence of the world is to be conceived as blind mechanism or as an intelligence that determines itself in accordance with purposes also comes down to it.[3]

Fatalism is opposed to freedom, and this opposition can be applied to the opposition between mechanism and teleology. Freedom is only possible in its concrete existence. In this sense, the mechanism is grounded in the immediacy of objectivity. This objective immediacy is the stupidity of Netflix. The algorithm based on big data would shape our preference of choice. By this rule we have no "freedom" to make our own choices. This iron cage of the teleo-technological mechanism is the principle of the platform media in this pandemic situation. Algorithmic machines such as Netflix, YouTube, and Facebook manage our taste for objects and serve as the possible formation of the present actuality. Ironically, these functions of technology, the mechanical totalization of objective data, make us believe that they are the essence of our lives.

Let us consider Hegel's use of teleology again here in order to reinstate the "purpose" of technology against the mechanization of life. According to Hegel, objective moments "stand in self-subsistent indifference as *objects each outside the other*, and as so related they possess the *subjective unity* of the concept only as *inner* or as *outer*."[4] Meanwhile, when the essential unity of objects is posited as "distinct from their self-subsistence" and the concept is subjective but supposed as "referring in and for itself to the objectivity, as *purpose*," it is teleology. Hegel continues to claim that "since purpose is the concept posited as within it referring to objectivity, and through itself sublating its defect of being subjective, the at first *external* purposiveness becomes, through the realization of the purpose, *internal*."[5] This argument sheds light on how purpose becomes an *idea*.

Hegel's teleology separates his idealism from that of other idealists, in particular, Berkeley and Kant, who regard mind and rational subjectivity as the origin of objects. For Hegel, whatever spiritual or ideal arises, further to Kant's self-consciousness, does not emerge at the beginning of thought (and being) but at the end of them. Hegel's spiritualism presupposes that the traumatic "education" of spirituality is extracted from the defects and errors of subjectivity. In this sense, Hegel's teleology allows us to think beyond the necessity built into mechanisms like Netflix. The purpose of the technology lies ironically in the flaw of its mechanism; that is, in the subjective hesitation, our reluctant pause before the choice. In other words, there is no final decision there, only undecidability, which has the absolute other not from the outside, but deferring differences from within. The Hegelian use of teleology aims at bringing in a meta-logical approach to the automatic algorithm.

RESISTANCES WITHIN MECHANISMS

In my opinion, Hegel's conception of teleology can be understood as the early consideration of today's automatization. Algorithmic categorizations such as Netflix reveal how mechanical necessity reserves internalized purpose. Even though a mechanism seems automatic, the hesitating decision-maker must be behind the machine. When the Gulf War broke out in 1990, Félix Guattari wrote "Towards a Post-Media Era," an essay in which he put forward the potential resistances in the mechanical categorization of media. He pondered the images of warfare on the television and stated that those media images of the event made us lift off into "an almost delirious universe of mass-media subjectivity."[6] "The growing power of software engineering," he argued, "does not necessarily lead to the power of Big Brother. In fact, it is way more cracked than it seems. It can blow up like a windshield under the impact of molecular alternative practices."[7]

Just what are these "molecular alternative practices" of media? In a Hegelian sense, they would be possible with the creation of purpose in the use of technology. For Guattari, "post-media" must practice expressive mediation against the mechanical representation of reality, since "the good old days of media" consisted of nothing less than scientific and positivist imagination. New teleo-technological situations have no powerful Big Brother in them; but they do contain many potential resistances. In this sense, what is urgently needed is to invent the "purpose" of post-media; in other words, a concept of it which stands in and for itself. The creation of self-determinate concepts is the main task for the "pure metaphysics" of "pure mechanism."

Following Henri Bergson, Gilles Deleuze's definition of his own philosophical purpose as pure metaphysics is appropriate for modern science and technology. It is not difficult to see the similarity between Deleuze's pure metaphysics and Hegel's teleology, but what separates Deleuze from Hegel is his understanding of negation. His rejection of Hegelian negation leads Deleuze to argue that Hegel's concept of conflict is another aspect of difference.[8] In line with Deleuze, Guattari emphasizes the "minor" use of technology. The concept of minority implies the affirmation of differences – that is, of those that are not subsumed by the generalization of the majority. The minor use of technology is nothing less than the creation of "inner purpose."

My accidental encounter with two different movies on Netflix and my critique of what I watched would be one of the possible practices that take up the experimental opportunity against mechanical necessity. What is to be done in this time of disaster capitalism is to affirm the contingency within mechanisms and to create the uncategorized purpose beyond the norms of algorithmic technology which are designed to modify our behaviour according to mechanical automatization. I believe that such resistances to technological affordances and the mechanical modification of desire will be the indefinite basis of politics against "pure capitalism."

NOTES

1 Naomi Klein, *The Shock Doctrine: The Rise of Disaster Capitalism* (New York: Metropolitan Books, 2007), 81.
2 Chang Liu, "My Boss Is Not Human (我的领导不是人)," *Caijing,* 11 January 2021, https://news.caijingmobile.com/article/detail/428729.
3 G.W.F. Hegel, *The Science of Logic,* trans. George Giovanni (Cambridge: Cambridge University Press, 2010), 651.
4 Ibid., 630.
5 Ibid., 640.
6 Félix Guattari, "Vers une ère post-média," in *Chimères* (1996), 16.
7 Ibid., 16–17.
8 Gilles Deleuze, *Difference and Repetition,* trans. Paul Patton (New York: Columba University Press, 1994), 222.

10

Free Speech

Natasha Lennard

In November 2019 Professor Jonathan Zimmerman spoke at the University of California, Davis, putatively to address the issue of free speech and censorship on university campuses.[1] Zimmerman, who has previously written with feverish concern for the well-being of young Trump voters at American colleges, framed the problem along an increasingly common spectrum in this debate: he suggested that a category mistake is being made when students and others demand that offensive speech be removed from campus discourse and that certain speakers be "de-platformed," or "no-platformed." By Zimmerman's lights, such demands are censorship driven by the "psychologizing of politics"; that is, your feelings are hurt (you "social justice snowflake"), and you conflate your psychic pain with a valid political stance around which to organize the permissibility or impermissibility of speech in your environment. We see a similar rhetoric play out when activists who amass to shut down far-right speakers are painted as foolishly impassioned, allowing their hot-blooded anger to overwhelm the political scene; the reasoned actor, we are told, allows even the most reprehensible figures to air their putrid ideologies in our midst, confident in the argumentative and persuasive strength of anti-racist, anti-nationalist rebuttals. "Politics and psychology don't play well together," said Zimmerman; the reasoned exchange of ideas, to be judged on their relative merits, is pitched against the oversensitive, unwieldy, apolitical and unphilosophic mob.

In such a schema, you would find me on the side of the mob: I stand with those students and organizers who, around the world, have made a point of shutting down racist far-right speakers and writers who have attempted to gain purchase on campuses and in cultural institutions.

For all its confidence in reasonability, Zimmerman's problematic of free and unfree speech is deeply flawed. A more stringently analytic and interrogative approach to speech, and what makes it free or not – indeed how it functions as speech at all – should lead one to see reason on the side of the "de-platformers." On the side of the free-speech absolutists, meanwhile, lies a quite fanciful and underthought understanding of no less than how language and meaning work. The category mistake is with those who, like Zimmerman, point to the issue of "psychologizing politics" but in fact mislocate the problem entirely. The more rigorous philosophy is on the side of the mob.

The most valid positions for expelling white-supremacist speech – which, to be sure, constitutes white-supremacist organizing – have been well made, again and again, most particularly by communities of colour, trans activists, and undocumented people who have attested to the immediate harm done to them when the presence of such voices is legitimized via public platform. These communities should no longer need to debate the mattering of their lives. I agree with this, marrow deep. But since their positions have been dismissed as over-emotional and anti-intellectual, I make this argument here to meet free-speech absolutists on their own proclaimed terms. Those who claim "reason" is on their side are in fact the purveyors of a near-religious and under-interrogated view of these language games.

I want here first to interrogate the assumptions implicit in the common concept of permissible and "free" speech deployed by defenders of the ability of far-right speakers to speak in public or publish in mainstream platforms. Then I will suggest an alternative, and I believe better, framework for thinking about the work done by certain types of speech; for this I rely upon (and support) philosopher Ludwig Wittgenstein's meaning-as-use approach,[2] along with some simple speech act theory, and I appeal to just a dash of proof from recent history. I hope to establish that a more robust discussion of speech acts and linguistic scenes supports arguments to shut down racist far-right speech in public; without this, a more just society can be neither performed nor practised.

Let me lay out some parameters; a necessary preamble, if you will. Or, if I am honest, a pre-emptive response to a tired counterargument. I am not interested in arguing here for any sort of changes to, or curtailment of, the First Amendment to the US Constitution. My argument pertains to how communities should better organize their thoughts and actions around the sorts of speech and assembly they enable and tolerate – how we might recognize our responsibilities for creating certain political realities in the spaces in which we live, learn, and work. The museum, the university administration, the newspaper, the social media company: these institutions can and do uphold stricter standards than the state – in some ways – when it comes to permitting or banning certain types of speech.

Furthermore, we must acknowledge that we are dealing with something slippery, dynamic and contextual: that is, speech. Yes, an institution could expand its set of banned symbols and phrases (Pepe the Frog as well as the swastika). But by changing the rules of permitted speech, the administration, or the state, would fail to arrest the dynamic of white-supremacist speech acts and their adaptability. Language games do have rules – if completely contravened, we fail to make meaningful speech together, producing mere noises – but the "rules" are exceedingly malleable. These games are not a chaotic free-for-all, but they are not chess either. If there is consensus around a new convention of usage among a linguistic community, we can keep talking; if not, communication fails. What gets to count as "correct play" in language is malleable but nonetheless dependent on a critical (enough) number of participants "playing along." As Wittgenstein knew, "the meaning of a word is its use in the language."[3]

* * *

Let me begin by recalling the words of US Supreme Court Justice Oliver Wendell Holmes Jr in his famed 1919 dissent in the case of Abrams v. United States – a text that has, perhaps more than any other, undergirded legal thinking around freedom of speech in America and beyond for the last century. "The best test of truth," wrote Holmes, "is the power of the thought to get itself accepted in the competition of the market."[4] Holmes was a pragmatist and a careful judicial thinker. But today we see his dissent reduced into an underthought premise for free-speech absolutism. Given the chance to compete with each other in this "marketplace of ideas," it suggests, the best ideas, indeed the truth, will win through; as such, it must be this marketplace, rather than some censorious authority or "mob," that determines which ideas are given a platform. The least and most we can and should do, according to such a framework, is to keep the marketplace open.

The overused market analogy – or market ideology – informs modern First Amendment doctrine, and constitutes the underexamined framework of today's free-speech debate. It is this framework, not the legal doctrine itself, that I take to task. It is based on a weak understanding of how speech, truth, and meaning works. Indeed, for a debate around speech in which the university campus is the terrain of contest, it is quite astounding how little theoretical attention has been given to the functioning of speech itself. It is as if decades – *centuries* – of philosophical work were somehow irrelevant in the face of only partially applicable, barely interrogated, liberal judicial ideology.

In July 2020, *Harper's Magazine* published a "Letter on Justice and Open Debate"[5] signed by over 150 writers, academics, and public figures – including anti-trans zealot J.K. Rowling, scholar-activist Noam Chomsky, novelist Margaret Atwood, and a host of exceedingly poor conservative and liberal thinkers like Steven Pinker and Malcolm Gladwell, alongside other paranoiac centrists who fear so-called cancel culture. Published during a potent moment of Black liberation struggle, when, finally, the institutional racism and whiteness of so many established media institutions was under the spotlight, the letter argued that speech was under threat. This threat came from the authoritarian impulses of Donald Trump, the letter noted, but its real focus was the "censoriousness" of the anti-racists and anti-fascists who dared demand that racism and anti-trans hate no longer be considered valid terrains of public debate. "It is now all too common to hear calls for swift and severe retribution in response to perceived transgressions of speech and thought," stated the letter – a most vicious deployment of the word "perceived." The letter echoes Holmes's dissent almost verbatim, as if his proposition were unquestionable: "The way to defeat bad ideas is by exposure, argument, and persuasion, not by trying to silence or wish them away."

A number of presumptions underlie this standardized approach to free speech. First, it presumes that this thing called the "market" is a fair judge of goodness and truth; that it is a fair organizer of justice. Such free-market fundamentalism is roundly decried, and is indeed laughable when applied to an economic context (and it is an economic analogy); in the aftermath of (just the latest) ferocious financial crisis, faith in the market as a fair arbiter is nothing but the near-religious preserve of the mega-rich – those who have benefited from the deeply unfair terrain that it is. Yet we continue to treat the market analogy as unproblematic when applied to speech and ideas; we have no grounds to do so and ample empirical basis to see the operations of "the marketplace of ideas" as equally rigged to favour existing power structures. Any claim otherwise finds itself in the terrain of what Jamaican philosopher Charles W. Mills calls "white ignorance"[6] – that well-fostered individualist epistemology whereby stories of truth-telling conveniently forget the facts of history. At one point, for example, in German-colonized South West Africa, white settlers demanded that in court only the testimony of seven African witnesses could outweigh evidence presented by a single white person. Or to raise more recent examples, we might point to the numerous Palestinian scholars, and any critics of Israeli state violence, who have been fired or denied the ability to speak through claims equating anti-Zionism, or indeed mild condemnation of Israel's extreme aggressions, with anti-Semitism. It has always been the case that the ideas "marketplace" has reflected existing systems of power. So tell me again about "best of truth" winning through by virtue of this market's determinations? Such pretenses, that there exists a neutral terrain on which ideas merely "compete" and that the "best" will win through, require a most fanatical lack of empiricism.

Second, the "free exchange of ideas" framework posits "truth" as something that is simply there, lying around to be found, to win the day. The framework thus ignores the dead, real, material conditions – the brutal hierarchies – that organize what gets to be truth. A more "critical" approach to truth-telling by no means denies the existence of verifiable facts but insists that attention is given to the "activity" of speech: who gets to do it, how, where, and to whom. This is not relativism with regard to truth; it is materialism, with a long-established history in the philosophy of science. A reckoning is in order with the limitations of facts in the face of disinterested power – the limitations of the language game of factual reporting in the face of the language game of white-supremacist propagandizing.

Third, and more to the point here, the absolutist model locates speech – the unit that is to be deemed permissible or not – in a specific way. There are "thoughts" that get themselves "accepted" into the marketplace of ideas or not. These "thoughts" are the bearers of truth, falsity, merit, or violence. Speech (whether verbal, written, or otherwise), then, is to be understood as that which conveys thoughts. There is the world, ideas about the world – which can be offensive or not, and true or not – and the speech that delivers those ideas. What we have here is a deeply rudimentary "conceptual" model of meaning, in which words simply attach to or represent the world (or fail to do so). Under such a static model, speech itself is merely a tool – equally available to all – with which we exchange ideas about the world. And if this is how meaning works, then certainly, an absolutist free-speech argument makes sense: it portrays the world and its truth as it is, while bad ideas about it – poor or incorrect representations of it in speech – will be shown to be false when held up against better representations of the truth of the world. Fear not, we are enjoined; by this model abhorrent ideas and theories, like race realism, will be felled by the sheer fact of being false, perverse representations of humanity and difference.

Funny, though, that race realism has not been felled, even though the concept has been so fully discredited. Maybe we just haven't delivered our "better," more just representations of the world with sufficient clarity. Maybe we simply need to debate harder. Or, just maybe, the model of communication we are relying on here is in itself false: maybe we are actually not talking about exchanging ideas about the world. Because, I submit, when far-right figures and groups gather and speak in the public sphere, on- and offline, they're not simply positing ideas about how they believe the world is and should be, offering their thoughts up to the marketplace of ideas to be earnestly considered and judged. Or, more precisely, they *are* describing the world as they believe it to be, but that is nevertheless the least relevant aspect of the speech acts at play in such a circum stance. It is high time we stopped perpetuating the myth that this is a debate about ... well, when it is appropriate to *debate*.

After all, a speech act is not simply the spoken representation of a thought about the world; it is the performance of an action. Like many speech acts, those performed by white supremacists in public are what the philosopher of language J.L. Austin called perlocutionary acts: that is, they are not so much organized around expressing the interiority of the speaker, or describing something, as they are designed to arouse a reaction in the listener – their force is their perlocutionary effect.[7] Here's a perlocutionary speech act: "I'm hungry!" I'm not telling you I'm hungry because I want you to simply know it. I'm not in a doctor's office after stomach complications, speaking in order to describe an internal experience. I'm telling you I'm hungry for the perlocutionary effect of you thinking you should get me food. A white nationalist's (false) statement that a "flood" of undocumented immigrants is spreading crime and taking resources is indeed offering a false description of the world, the falseness of which can be and has been pointed out. But the speech act is more significant in its perlocutionary force and effect: the utterance doesn't function primarily as a description, to be tested for truth or falsity; the listener (if a white European) is being told to feel threatened, and if non-white, non-European, is, in turn, being threatened by being named as a threat external to the direct audience. What is going on here, when these speech acts are enacted, is not (again borrowing from Wittgenstein) best read through "the language game of reporting." The speech acts of expressing and spreading fascistic, white supremacist desires are not parts of the language game we might call the "open exchange of ideas."

The most obvious response is: Why not simply respond with better speech acts? "Speak truth to perlocutionary effect," if you will. I want specifically to address why racist, homophobic, transphobic, anti-immigrant speech acts – *qua* speech acts – are not best combatted through *debate*. On the level of speech acts, I borrow from feminist philosopher Mary Kate McGowan. McGowan has made some flawed criticisms of sex work and pornography,[8] but I find her work useful here. She notes that to try to remove racism, misogyny, transphobia, and other oppressive speech from a linguistic scene is like trying to "unring a bell"[9] – it is much easier to introduce sexist and racist presuppositions into a conversation than it is to exorcise them. They are what are known as "exercitive speech acts"[10] – they determine what sort of actions or behaviours are permissible in a given domain. The police make a lot of exercitive speech acts; as do judges, umpires, and referees. But there are all kinds of other quotidian examples. A group of acquaintances may be having dinner, and one attendee starts talking about sex, so everyone feels permitted to talk about sex. There's no going back to the point before the topic was raised. But the stakes of the introduction of oppressive speech into a space, meanwhile, have been raised by the pernicious matter at hand.

Just "raising questions" about racist pseudoscience, as well as outright white-supremacist speech, involves illocutionary acts (that is, speech acts that perform deeds when uttered, like promising, declaring, or commanding) that enact what McGowan calls "oppressive permissibility facts."[11] From the speech acts of Richard Spencer's invocation of "white pride" and Milo Yiannopoulos's mockery of trans students, to Charles Murray's suggestion that white men are intellectually superior, or that of Senator Tom Cotton urging that the military be deployed against Black American protesters – these all enact, even if not explicitly, the permissibility of oppression in the environment in which they are spoken. The perlocutionary effect of Trump's racist speech – that is, the attendant huge spike in white-supremacist hate crimes – should make this clear. And again, conversations are asymmetrically pliable: there's a general asymmetry between verbally making something salient (by which I mean noticeable) as part of a linguistic scene or terrain, and verbally making something unsalient. Think of trying to unring a bell, or put toothpaste back into the tube. Calls for the free exchange of ideas, appeals to capital-T truth, wholly fail to reckon with asymmetric pliability and the introduction of oppressive permissibility facts. That is to say, free speech absolutism again fails in its understanding of how speech works. Those who have felt the brute force of this "introduction of oppressive permissibility facts" – that is, the vile lived reality of racism – don't need speech act theory to understand this. It is shameful that so many cultural, institutional, and educational gatekeepers still do.

Let us look at the language games at play in the following example. When, in response to the many, many executions, beatings, and cagings of Black people by police and the criminal justice system, thousands rose up to assert "Black Lives Matter!" the call was for a truth that has not been – has never been – instantiated in the United States or the West more generally: Black lives have not been permitted to matter. In response, the worst reactionaries and most stupid centrists asked why we could not instead make the call, "All lives matter!" It is a true statement, to be sure: all lives do matter. But under the current and violent order of things, all lives don't get to matter; by parrying the specificity of Black lives and functioning as a rejoinder, the utterance, albeit true, commits its own violence. The meaning of a statement is in its use, and the call is deployed not in the language game of describing the mattering of lives, but in the maintenance of brutal, racist hierarchies in which Black lives don't get to matter. "Black Lives Matter!," as a speech act, is not uttered *primarily* in the service of description either; it is a demand, to be repeated until it doesn't need saying anymore.

I am interested in these language games of resistance and how we play them. That is why I, and many others, use the word "fascist" to describe Donald Trump, his adviser Stephen Miller, the alt-right Reform UK (née Brexit) Party leader Nigel Farage, and the German Alternative für Deutschland, among others. We could simply call them far-right nationalists and racists, and we do that, too. Those who claim that these figures do not fit a formal definition of "fascism," however, miss the fact that fascism is a family-resemblance concept – and these characters and groups certainly share in "a network of similarities" with what was historically described as "fascist." And many of us who use the term "fascism" today do so in order to invite an anti-fascist response, a response of resolute intolerance to the fascistic constellations we are seeing. This too is a speech act, not simply a description – an aggressive and ethical move to draw and redraw the boundaries of what we might call "fascist" as we go.

It is worth noting that the contemporary far right, metastasizing online, often uses the pliability of meaning to its advantage. Consider, if you will, the "okay" hand symbol (index finger and thumb held in a ring): far-right trolls laughed at liberals who "fell" for the supposed hoax of believing the "okay" hand sign to be a white-supremacist gesture. But since it was white supremacists who kept "okaying" in photos, it turns out the social justice snowflakes were correctly observing the addition of a new hate symbol to the lexicon through the far right's collective use. In response to alleged political correctness gone too far, the vile alt-right radio host Paul Joseph Watson once tweeted, "Wearing a sombrero is not racist, you utter dolt. It's a fucking hat." Against this sort of disingenuous appeal to "factual" meaning as a cover for racism, we can say to those playing Watson's game: "Look, you utter fascists, use is meaning – it's not just a fucking hat!"

One might respond: "But hey, it's not like far-right speakers today would be introducing white-supremacist ideology by extolling it publicly; these aren't new ideas! They undergird the history of Europe and the United States. So since the bell has been rung, and rung and rung, we can't pretend never to have heard it." This rebuttal, however, misses the difference between citationality – the ability to cite and discuss a given discourse without restating or reasserting its claims – and each new (oppressive) speech act. I am not suggesting that we not talk about and discuss white-supremacist ideology; we are doing it now, and to do so requires white-supremacist speech to be in some sense citationally available, so that we can know what it has looked like, currently looks like, and how it persists and changes and warps. But this does not mean that speech acts of the far right on campuses, online, and in public are thus useful in exposing us to these ideas. Rather, they are overexposed: their speech acts function only to introduce oppressive permissibility facts into a given locale, a given community. And this is precisely the language game that must not be entertained. Indeed, the work of vigorous, loud, disruptive, sometimes-confrontational protest is deployed precisely to ensure that the insidious language game of enacted white-supremacist permissibility facts is deemed too intolerable to play.

NOTES

1 Jonathan Zimmerman, professor of history of education at the University of Pennsylvania (2019), lecture delivered at the University of California, Davis, 14 November 2019.

2 Ludwig Wittgenstein, *Philosophical Investigations* (Oxford: Basil Blackwell, 1953).

3 Ibid., 43.

4 Justice Oliver Wendell Holmes in Abrams *v.* United States, 250 U.S. 616, the United States Supreme Court, 1919.

5 Elliot Ackerman et al., "A Letter on Justice and Open Debate," *Harper's Magazine,* 7 July 2020, https://harpers.org/a-letter-on-justice-and-open-debate/.

6 Charles W. Mills, "White Ignorance," in *Race and Epistemologies of Ignorance*, eds., Shannon Sullivan and Nancy Tuana (Albany: State University of New York Press, 2007), 11–38.

7 John L. Austin, *How to Do Things with Words* (Cambridge: Harvard University Press, 2003).

8 Ishani Maitra and Mary Kate McGowan, "The Limits of Free Speech: Pornography and the Question of Coverage," *Legal Theory* 13 (2007): 41–68.

9 Mary Kate McGowan, "Oppressive Speech," *Australasian Journal of Philosophy* 87, no. 3 (2009): 389–407.

10 Ibid.

11 Ibid.

PART THREE

Outspoken Policies

Affirmative Politics:
Beyond the Rhetoric of Lament

Rosi Braidotti

Our era is toxic with negativity. A refrain about decline and decay, death, extinction, and the end of just about everything circulates in all kinds of variations across contemporary culture. It has plunged whinging and complaining to new lows of repetition, reaching problematic degrees of popularity. This refrain constitutes a populist variation on an old apocalyptic genre, which I call: the rhetoric of the self-pitying lament.

Monopolized and manipulated by conservative political forces, this rhetoric for the most part voices discontent that manifests as disenchantment and anger. The feeling that the status quo is under threat fuses easily with white-masculine rage, initiating a chain reaction that includes unchecked misogyny, triumphant sexism, and sexual violence; homo- and transphobia; racism, antisemitism, Islamophobia, xenophobia, hatred of immigrants and asylum-seekers, and a fatal attraction for illiberal governance. Whiteness and masculinity emerge, therefore, as major factors in creating the kind of existential risks the rest of the world's population has to deal with. The attitude they generate spreads a vituperative hatred of otherness – the unfamiliar, the unexpected – which fits the category of micro-fascism defined as an ethical deficiency, a relational deficit, and a political failure.[1]

THE POSTHUMAN CONVERGENCE

The sense of things coming to an end is admittedly fuelled by ample empirical evidence about the emergencies our planet is facing in an era marked by what I call "the posthuman convergence."[2] This juncture is framed by the simultaneous occurrence of the Fourth Industrial Revolution[3] and the Sixth Extinction;[4] fast-moving technological advances are matched by the acceleration of catastrophic environmental degradation and socio-economic inequalities. Confronted with fractures and systemic violence, posthuman convergence designs emotional and psychic landscapes swept by swinging moods. They trigger an alternation of conflicting emotions such as hope and despair, excitement and anxiety. But above them all, the rhetoric of the self-pitying lament rules.

This rhetoric of complaint is as popular on the left as on the right of the political spectrum. On the right, the populist tradition stresses sacralized notions of cultural authenticity, which replace or reinforce appeals to blood and soil. Cultural essentialism – or ethno-nationalism – in the guise of civic pride, is the refrain of today's right-wing populism. On the left of the political spectrum, social classes devastated by decades of economic decline and enforced austerity have endorsed the public expression of "whitelash": white people's – mostly men's – anger, producing a virulent form of neo-nationalist populism. All populists capitalize on the frustrations and fears of those who were impoverished by the fallout of economic globalization, thus adding a new chapter to the long history of the politics of resentment. They all mobilize against the post-nationalist potential of the European Union, which remains anathema for right- as for left-wing extremists.[5]

Intellectual and academic debates experience the same phenomenon, in the form of a well-funded and carefully orchestrated sequence of "culture wars." In Europe, public intellectual and literary figures on the right and left of the spectrum have canonized the rhetoric of lament. Michel Houellebecq and Alain Finkielkraut in France and Thilo Sarrazin in Germany lead the crusade, just as Samuel Huntington had done in the 1990s in the United States.[6] They specifically target what they perceive as the civilizational decline of Europe in relation to Islam. This self-flagellation seems to be especially strong in French culture, where the figure of the intellectual has historically played a significant public role in the making of a secular and Republican civic space. Thus, Eric Zemmour writes about the "suicide" of French cultural excellence, and in the Netherlands the far-right politician Thierry Baudet waxes lyrical about the superiority of "Borealism" and the Nordic races.[7]

But spirits are not exactly high in the progressive rank and file of the philosophical community either, with Bruno Latour commenting ambivalently about the end of critique itself – insofar as he never believed in it to begin with. Alain Badiou, on the other hand, complains about the theoretical impotence of what's left of the left, while Andreas Malman regrets that not everybody is a Leninist these days.[8] Slavoj Žižek, after supporting Trump against the feminist, anti-racist wishy-washy liberals, preaches a return to Hegel as a life raft in the choppy seas of posthuman convergence.[9] Former liberal Mark Lilla of Columbia University attacks all other liberals for giving in to identity politics and political correctness, while Jordan Peterson from Toronto attacks as an enemy of *the* people anybody who expresses sympathy for liberal causes.[10] The lament is the defining feature of the discourses of nativist populist movements, as exemplified by Steve Bannon as the dark prince of neo-apocalyptic alt-right thinking.

It is difficult not to see this self-pitying lament as the emerging posture of Western males contemplating the spectacle – or even just the possibility – of their own socio-economic loss of unearned privileges. The tendency is to scapegoat feminists, LGBTQ+ people and Black, Indigenous, and people of colour, as well as asylum-seekers and Muslim people in general. European populism is proto-fascist in orientation and genealogy, but it is also a bundle of contradictions held together by inveterate sexism and racism. On the one hand populists claim to embrace Christianity as the alleged core of European civilization, making concessions to Christian fundamentalism, family values, homo- and transphobia, and anti-feminism in general. On the other hand, populists flirt with anti-Christian paganism and an utter lack of charity and compassion. Catholic (Salvini, Orbán, Bolsonaro, and so forth), Protestant (Baudet, Rees-Mogg, American Evangelicals), Hindu (Modi), and Orthodox (Putin) populist leaders manipulate religion for purposes of exclusion, xenophobia, and Islamophobia.

These "populists from above" are leading the new cultural wars from positions of great power, and combine visceral anti-feminism with ancestral anti-abortion natalist politics and xenophobia.[11] Their aggressive nativism has been openly condemned by Pope Francis and the religious leaders of the very churches they claim to defend, because it encourages violent neocolonial crusades against the many unwanted "others." These neo-nationalist politicians have triggered a series of political backlashes that endanger the hard-won progress made by feminist and LGBTQ+ people. But they also jeopardize democratic proceedings in general, confronting us with the spectre of what Isabelle Stengers calls "the coming barbarism."[12] The self-appointed crusaders of the West are also the enemies of liberalism, industrial modernity, and democracy. Resolutely reactionary, they claim to be pre-Enlightenment thinkers and propose their own mythologized reading of the classical sources of Western culture as a homogenous religious and cultural continuum that they call "humanity." Rejecting representative democracy and social-contract theory, their propose to draw political legitimacy directly from the people. And the people are always and only One – rooted in a sacralized notion of soil and blood. Always the same old micro-fascist refrain.

THE ANTHROPOCENE AS EUROCENTRIC PANIC

In Anthropocene scholarship, the sense of apocalyptic panic is overwhelming. Mainstream Anthropocene-oriented scholarship is awash with angst as industrialized, developed, and technologically advanced humanity perceives itself as standing on the edge of a precipice and on the verge of extinction.[13] In this culturally specific conception, the future of the human is now preoccupying vast numbers of social commentators and philosophers.[14] The mood is generally sombre.

Popular culture is ready to magnify it. Hollywood and the streaming platforms have been quick to take up this morose mood and commodify it, turning catastrophe into a highly profitable entertainment genre: disaster movies, extinction series, posthuman futures. They are a cruelly optimistic variation on what is becoming known as "Apocalypse Chic." Extinction is cool, even as the planet gets hotter and hotter, and the new theoretical field known as "Collapsology" is in full expansion.[15] These catastrophic climate-change narratives and scenarios are, according to Gry Ulstein and Mahlu Mertens, overwhelmingly white, Eurocentric, and masculine.[16] It follows, therefore, that the key question – to which I will return in my conclusion – is the following: who are "we" that comprise a humanity at risk? Whose pain and anxiety is being expressed here?

The Eurocentric rhetoric of the self-pitying lament in relation to climate change expresses profound irresponsibility and immaturity. It is all the more objectionable considering that almost 50 per cent of global emissions are produced by the wealthiest 10 per cent of the world's population, but the impact of these emissions is hurting the poorest first and worst, especially in the global South. This is why I have been calling for a strong, activist posthuman feminist position to replace the rhetoric of lament with affirmative politics and develop some decolonial critical consciousnesses about climate change.[17] One thing is clear: the project of Western industrial modernity, which deployed a fossil fuel–led model of extractive economies and colonial economic growth and assumed an unlimited exploitation of "natural" resources, has shown its limitations. This capitalist, colonial, and patriarchal model, which is the root cause of ecological depletion, is inextricably linked to the colonial appropriation of land, culture, and resources from Indigenous people, their enslavement, and their dehumanization. To become aware of such historical responsibilities – at long last – should be greeted as an opportunity to develop adequate knowledge of the abuses of the Western world and to atone ethically and politically for them. The rhetoric of lament fails on both scores: it blurs the epistemological insight and misses the ethical challenge, mistaking them instead as a self-centred crisis of legitimation. Through such a sleight of hand, neocolonial populist politics perpetuates the willful ignorance and crass arrogance of the past, reducing its own capacity for moral and social growth.

The sense of panic triggered by mainstream Western discussions of climate change, the Anthropocene, and species extinction has been viewed with justified skepticism by Black, decolonial, and especially Indigenous critical thinkers, LGBTQ+ people, and feminists. In these activist movements, the mood is both upbeat and more community-minded. Many have pointed out that First Nations people have already experienced the devastation of their lands and cultures through the violence of colonization.[18] As Déborah Danowski and Eduardo Viveiros de Castro poignantly expressed it: "for the native people of the Americas, the end of the world already happened – five centuries ago. To be exact, it began on October 12, 1492."[19] Black and Indigenous thinkers, like many non-Western philosophers, consequently call for a more critical account of the climate-change emergency, one that allows for decolonial perspectives and anti-racist approaches. From a decolonial perspective, these fits of "white panic" signal the return of colonial violence upon those most responsible for it. The Anthropocene in this respect is the return of nature and its intrusion into the dominant, Western, Christian, capitalist, civilizational matrix.

My critical posthuman stance joins the activists' call for solidarity and community action and also argues for a more balanced assessment of the fallout of the posthuman convergence. In my posthuman analysis I have moreover pointed out that, in spite of increasing mobilization on the part of progressive political forces, there is no evidence at present that the dominant economic and civilizational Western economic and cultural model is being questioned. For instance, in April 2020 – in the midst of the coronavirus pandemic – US president Trump signed an executive order allowing American companies to mine resources from the moon and asteroids in outer space. This move expressed undying support for extraction economies, as well as supreme contempt for environmental politics, let alone International Law. But Trump's executive order – which incidentally was immediately confirmed by the incoming Biden administration – also encouraged partnerships between the federal government and the private sector. Space exploration nowadays is dominated by the private capital of tycoons like Jeff Bezos, Elon Musk, and Richard Branson, who are keen to mine extra-terrestrial space for resources, including water and key minerals.

All autocrats being the same, however, Trump's intergalactic ambitions are not unique as an expression of latter-day imperialism. In August 2007, two teams of Russian explorers and researchers travelling in mini-submarines planted their country's flag on the seabed 4,200 metres below the North Pole. The purpose of this extraordinary gesture was to further Moscow's claims to ownership of the Arctic region and to confirm Putin's territorial claim to the sea, currently administered by the International Seabed Authority and regulated by International Law. The melting of the polar ice caps has opened the possibility of new shipping and trade routes at the North Pole, thereby intensifying the competition among these neocolonial powers. So, contemporary autocratic leaders continue to uphold a failed and murderous model of neocolonial capitalist growth, and even aim to expand it, with no concern for the risks, costs, and injustices it entails. The same contempt and indifference for the human and non-human risks and costs was displayed during the COVID-19 pandemic. Both climate change denial and COVID-19 denial are defining features of contemporary populist negativity. Again, previously critical intellectuals are not immune from this regressive behaviour. Giorgio Agamben, for instance, turned coronavirus-denialist and, after disputing the lethal character of the COVID-19 epidemic,[20] joined forces with fellow Italian critical philosopher Massimo Cacciari to defend the rights of the "no vax" movement.[21] Attacking public health measures as the arbitrary expression of a despotic state of emergency, Agamben underestimated the threat the virus represents and ignores the heavy toll it has already taken in terms of human lives.

Commentators have noted that the countries which, so far, have benefited from the most effective pandemic-managing governance appear to be those led by women. That is the case for Finland (Sanna Marin), Iceland (Katrin Jakobsdóttir), Denmark (Mette Frederiksen), New Zealand (Jacinda Ardern), Taiwan (Tsai Ing-wen), and Germany (Angela Merkel). Cynthia Enloe raises the obvious question: "Are women-led governments both more civically responsible and more likely to inspire trust, and thus the public's compliance with health rules, than are governments led by men?" And conversely, are the toxic versions of masculinity circulating in the anti-lockdown position of the political right during the pandemic – particularly "cavalier masculinity, mercurial masculinity, arrogant masculinity, clownish masculinity, militarized masculinity" – most likely to let down public trust during a public health crisis? And with what consequences?[22]

Not to care for the pain of others – human and non-human others – is a form of callousness and ethical incompetence that accommodates brutal structural social and economic inequalities with advanced high technologies. The logic and the rhetoric of the self-pitying lament expresses a narrow sense of self-centred vulnerability, which seems to assume that the only pain that matters in the world is white people's and especially white men's pain.[23] It breeds a sense of powerlessness that poisons the public sphere, producing painful fractures. It envisages technological programs of human enhancement, but also accepts the "need" to sacrifice entire sectors of the earth's population, both human and non-human. In a morally bankrupt display of its necro-political soul, late capitalism is planning economic expansion for a few and managed decline for most of the others. A necro-political logic of sacrifice is being deployed which makes entire sectors of populations disposable and hence more mortal than others. What is being installed is a system of sexualized, racialized, and naturalized selection of who gets to survive, and who is left to perish.

WHY WE NEED A FEMINIST
AFFIRMATIVE ETHICS

Critical thinkers usually have to think against their times – in spite of their times, but also out of concern for them. This insight rings painfully true in the midst of the posthuman convergence, with its heady combination of stupefying technological progress, stultifying environmental degradation, and widespread human and non-human suffering.

Fortunately, the regression is counteracted by multiple resistance movements that are also making headlines and redrawing the maps of political activism the world over, notably BLM and anti-racist groups, new feminist and LGBTQ+ movements, and transnational environmental justice movements. A feminist affirmative ethics brings an active and tonic response against twisted discourses and practices of recrimination and self-righteous lament. Affirmation is neither acquiescence nor shallow optimism, but rather a critical praxis whose goal is the collective transformation of negativity. Resetting a basic agenda of empathy, generic care for humans and non-humans, and solidarity, a feminist politics of respect and equality seems an obvious place to start. But it looks further, arguing that the same conditions that cause our concerns also contain the potential to bring solutions.

An affirmative ethics states that we have to be worthy of our times in order to resist them, in a collaborative construction of alternative ways of "being-in-this-together." The critical spirit of feminist activists, in their great diversity, finds its creative inspiration again, so as to cope with social and political challenges of the posthuman convergence. Adequate understanding guides the ethics: "we" need to acknowledge the pain and disenchantment, learning from our mistakes and those of others, in order to move forward and build a new political praxis. Negativity, like all passions, is strong and binding. The binding power generated by the collective expression of negative emotions and violent passions such as hatred, intolerance, rage, cynicism, and opportunism contains, however, an affirmative nucleus. It shows our mutual interdependence and our ability to affect and be affected by one another. To acknowledge this deep interrelational affective bond of empathy, care, and compassion is the beginning of a new wisdom that sustains affirmative ethics. It is a form of ontological generosity.

The rhetoric of lament results in a reactive composition of a community – "we" – a people bonded, in this particular instance, by negative affects and relations. The political intervention consists in injecting different ethical flows into this equation, fighting the inadequate rendition of the situation – the untruths, fake news, and injustices – by means of arguments and persuasion. Speaking truth to power, both in classrooms and in the public sphere, mobilizes knowledge-production practices for the sake of reaching a more adequate understanding of the negative conditions that oppress us. It is even more important to foster affirmative and positive propositions and relations.

It is important, therefore, to advance a radical critique of this hasty recomposition of a "we" as *the* people bonded in fear. We need to move beyond dialectical oppositions between us and them, beyond the logic of violent antagonism, to develop an operational politics of affirmation. This is not a simple or pain-free process, of course, but anger alone is not a project, though it can result in populist mobilizations. Anger needs to be transformed into the power to act; it needs to become a constitutive force addressed not only "against" but also "in favour of" something. Negative passions like resentment are conducive to violence and paralysis, not to change. More than ever we need forms of political opposition that are rich in alternatives, concrete in propositions, and guided by an ethics of affirmation. This requires accurate political cartographies of the power relations that we inhabit and by which we are structured. Precisely because it feels at times as if we are living in the pit of negativity, surrounded by dishonesty and violence, we will have to cultivate the ethics of affirmation.

Crucial to this process is the question: who and how many are "we"? "We" may well be a reactive formation, a resistance against the alliance of neoliberalism with multiple fundamentalisms. But in order to become transformative, it must act affirmatively. We need to compose together a plane of agreement about what our shared hopes and aspirations are; we need to compare notes on what kind of world we want to build together as an alternative. Critique and creation work hand in hand. Thus, while denouncing the exacerbation of misogyny, racism, inequality, authoritarianism, and cynicism in the present political context, I want to repeat the question that guides my posthuman project: to what extent can "we" say that "we" are in *this* together?

Mindful that "human" never was a unitary category to begin with, but rather a term that indexes access to rights and entitlements, I want to plead for materially embedded and embodied differential perspectives that honour the internal fractures and systemic contradictions of our respective locations as well as our common belonging to a shared planetary and social destiny. By multiplying the degrees and qualities of differently embedded and embodied subjects to include both organic and non-organic non-humans, this diversified materialist approach will bring the basic concepts of feminism into a posthuman perspective.

A posthuman ethics of affirmation supports the formation of a heterogeneous subject who argues forcefully that, yes, "we-are-in-this-together-but-we-are-not-one-and-the-same." Accounting for the heterogeneity while being moved to act together is of the essence in a political context dominated by the rhetoric of lament that risks becoming the expression of white male Eurocentric angst. It is time to listen to the sexualized, racialized, and naturalized others. And to learn some humility.

Posthuman feminism applies a practical mix of posthumanist and post-anthropocentric measures to construct solidarity, while avoiding hasty returns to pan-humanity. The alternative is an affirmative ethics of heterogeneous transversal assemblages. In the midst of our technologically mediated social relations, and in response to the paranoid rhetoric of our post-truth democratic leaders, how can we work together to construct critical posthuman subjects as an affirmative ethical and political practice? How can we work toward socially sustainable horizons of hope through resistance? The answer is in the doing, in the praxis of composing alliances and transversal connections, and through engaging in difficult conversations on what troubles us. "We" need to create new social imaginaries and ignite affirmative political passions that relay the eternal battle cry of the margins: don't agonize, organize, because there is just so much that needs to be done.

NOTES

1 Gilles Deleuze, *Spinoza: Practial Philosophy* (San Francisco: City Lights Books, 1988); Rosi Braidotti, *Transpositions* (Cambridge: Polity Press, 2006); forthcoming text by Rosi Braidotti and Rick Dolphijn.

2 Rosi Braidotti, *The Posthuman* (Cambridge: Polity Press, 2013); Rosi Braidotti, *Posthuman Knowledge* (Cambridge: Polity Press, 2019).

3 Klaus Schwab, "The Fourth Industrial Revolution," *Foreign Affairs*, 12 December 2015, https://www.foreignaffairs.com/articles/2015-12-12/fourth-industrial-revolution.

4 Elizabeth Kolbert, *The Sixth Extinction* (New York: Henry Holt, 2014).

5 Jürgen Habermas, *The Postnational Constellation* (Cambridge: Polity Press, 2001); Rosi Braidotti, *Nomadic Theory* (New York: Columbia University Press, 2011).

6 Michel Houellebecq, *Submission* (Paris: Flammarion, 2015); Alain Finkielkraut, *L'identité malheureuse* (Paris: Stock, 2013); Thilo Sarrazin, *Deutschland schafft sich ab* (Munchen: Deutsche Verlags-Anstalt, 2010).

7 Eric Zemmour, *Le suicide français* (Paris: Albin Michel, 2014).

8 Bruno Latour, "Why Has Critique Run Out of Steam?" *Critical Inquiry* 30, no. 2 (2004): 225–48; Alain Badiou, "Our Contemporary Impotence," *Radical Philosophy* 181 (2013): 40–3; Andreas Malman, *Fossil Capital* (London: Verso Books, 2016).

9 Marcus Browne, "Slavoj Žižek: Trump Is Really a Centrist Liberal," *The Guardian*, 28 April 2016, https://www.theguardian.com/books/2016/apr/28/slavoj-zizek-donald-trump-is-really-a-centrist-liberal.

10 Mark Lila, *The Once and Future Liberal* (New York: HarperCollins, 2017); Jordan Peterson, *12 Rules for Life: An Antidote to Chaos* (Toronto: Penguin Random House, 2018).

11 Arjun Appadurai, "The Revolt of the Elites," *IWM POST* 125 (2020): 19.

12 Isabelle Stengers, *In Catastrophic Times: Resisting the Coming Barbarism* (Open Humanities Press, 2015).

13 Roy Scranton, *Learning to Die in the Anthropocene* (San Francisco: City Light Books, 2015); Claire Colebrook, *Death of the Posthuman* (Ann Arbor: Open Humanities Press/University of Michigan Press, 2014); Arthur Kroker, *Exits to the Posthuman Future* (Cambridge: Polity, 2014); Toby Orb, *The Precipice: Existential Risk and the Future of Humanity* (London: Bloomsbury, 2020).

14 Francis Fukuyama, *Our Posthuman Future: Consequences of the Biotechnological Revolution* (London: Profile Books, 2002); Jürgen Habermas, *The Future of Human Nature* (Cambridge: Polity, 2003). Peter Sloterdijk, "Rule for the Human Zoo: A Response to the Letter on Humanism," *Environment and Planning D: Society and Space* 27, no. 1 (2009): 12–28; Pope Francis, *Encyclical Letter 'Laudato si': On Care for Our Common Home* (Rome: Vatican Press, 2015).

15 Pablo Servigne and Raphael Stevens, *How Everything Can Collapse* (Cambridge: Polity Press, 2020).

16 Mahlu Mertens and Gry Ulstein, "Decolonizng the Cli-Fi Corpus," *Collateral: Online Journal for Cross-Cultural Close Reading*, 26 November 2020, http://www.collateral-journal.com/index.php?cluster=26.

17 Rosi Braidottti, *Posthuman Knowledge* (Cambridge: Polity Press, 2019); Rosi Braidotti, *Posthuman Feminism* (Cambridge: Polity Press, 2021).

18 Bruce Clarke, *Posthuman Metamorphosis* (New York: Fordham University Press, 2008); Zoe Todd, "An Indigenous Feminist's Take on

the Ontological Turn: 'Ontology' Is Just Another Word for Colonialism,"
Journal of Historical Sociology 29, no. 1 (2016): 4–22; Kyle P. Whyte,
"Is It Colonial Déjà Vu? Indigenous Peoples and Climate Injustice," in
*Humanities for the Environment: Integrating Knowledges, Forging New
Constellations of Practice*, eds. Joni Adamson, Michael Davis, and Hsinya
Huang (Abingdon-on-Thames: Earthscan Publications, 2016), 88–104.

19 Déborah Danowski and Eduardo Viveiros de Castro, *The Ends of the
World* (Cambridge: Polity Press, 2017), 105.

20 Giorgio Agamben, "L'invenzione di un'epidemia," *Quodlibet,* 26 February
2020, www.quodlibet.it/giorgio-agamben-l-invenzione-di-un-epidemia;
see also www.journal-psychoanalysis.eu/coronavirus-and-philosophers/
for an English translation.

21 Giorgio Agamben and Massimo Cacciari, "A proposito del decreto sul
'green pass,'" IISF, 26 July 2021, https://www.iisf.it/index.php/progetti/
diario-della-crisi/massimo-cacciari-giorgio-agamben-a-proposito-del-decreto-
sul-green-pass.html.

22 Cynthia Enloe, "Femininity and the Paradox of Trust Building in
Patriarchies during COVID-19," *Signs,* autumn, 2020, http://signsjournal.
org/covid/.

23 Naomi Klein, *On Fire: The Burning Case for a Green New Deal* (London:
Allen Lane, 2019).

12

Anarchafeminist Manifesto

Chiara Bottici

If Black women were free, it would mean that everyone else would have
to be free since our freedom would necessitate the destruction of all
the systems of oppression.

The Combahee River Collective

We live under a global "menocracy." Worldwide and individually,
women are oppressed. At a time when information, capital, and
viruses travel instantly around the world, when the fate of a few
islands on one side of the globe depends on the carbon dioxide emissions on the other, we cannot pretend we did not know, and so we
know. What do we know? We know that women are politically,
economically, socially, and sexually oppressed.

There are many tools by which men exercise their privilege, but
a useful, although temporary list includes the following: i) death,
ii) the state, iii) capital, iv) the imaginal. Death, because women are
the object of a worldwide gendercide; the state, because the sovereign
state is an instrument of the sovereign sex; capital, because acquiring
it exploits women more than it exploits men; and the imaginal,
because images that are detrimental to women populate and prolifer-
ate in the global imaginary.

WOMEN'S GENDERCIDE

A global war is being waged against women. Why are there more men
than women on the planet, despite the fact that women tend to live
longer? Where have all the missing girls gone? The "missing girls" are

counted not in the hundreds, or thousands, but in the millions. It is currently estimated that at least 126 million girls are missing from the global population as a consequence of sex-selective abortion, infanticide, and inequalities of childcare.[1]

Although the administration of death via denial of birth is perhaps the most powerful biopolitical tool of the global menocracy, violence against women's bodies does not stop after birth. Currently, at least 35 per cent of women worldwide have experienced physical and/or sexual violence.[2] The war against women is also evident in statistics regarding forced displacements; women and girls account for 71 per cent of the global business. When it comes to kidnapping and forcing human beings from one geographical location to another with the purpose of either sexual exploitation, forced labour, or a combination of both, it is largely women who pay the highest price with their own bodies. One may think that by keeping women at home one would be able to protect them. But as the coronavirus pandemic clearly showed, homes are only safe for the first sex: as the lockdown went on, gender violence went up.[3]

Where are men in all these numbers? Where are men in all these acts of sex-selective abortion, female infanticide, and female homicides? They are making sure the "first sex"[4] will remain the first for quite some time to come. Even in contexts where the oppression of women is hidden over by an official recognition of equality between the sexes, women and LGTBQ+ people are still the second sex – and not only because they are the object of a gendercide.

Thus, together with trans- and queer theory's groundbreaking work aimed at questioning gender binaries and identification practices, it is important to vindicate once again the need for a form of feminism that opposes the oppression of people who are perceived as women and who are discriminated against precisely on that basis. Anarchafeminism and queer theory are also bedfellows insofar as they both question processes of normalization that lead to exclusion and hierarchy, including those rooted in gender and sex itself: for both of them, the old anarchist motto "the outcast is my enemy" holds true. True to the spirit, if not the letter of queer theory, anarchafeminism means feminism without an *arche*, that is feminism without hierarchies – including sexual, economic, political, and racial hierarchies. We cannot fight one form of oppression without fighting all others at the same time, for all forms of oppression inhabit the same house – all forms of belief that some people are superior to others, and that this superiority justifies their domination over others.[5] We can thus say that to the extent that there are outcasts in our society, or bodies that are oppressed and discriminated against because of their sex or gender, there will be a need for an anarchafeminist cry.

Against gendercide and all forms of violence against the second sex, we anarchafeminists call for the liberation of all women. Not one less! Either all, or none of us will be free.

THE SOVEREIGN STATE AS AN INSTRUMENT OF THE SOVEREIGN SEX

One of the main instruments through which men perpetrate their privilege and make sure they remain the sovereign sex is the state. Cisgendered men are the sovereign sex because, like sovereign states, they do not have to recognize any sex superior to theirs. The state has always been the tool whereby a minority ruled over the majority,[6] but few have noticed the intrinsically gendered dimension of that formidable power. The world is currently divided into 195 sovereign states, and there is no habitable piece of land that is not covered by a state. This means that we are forced to live under state rule, which is tantamount to saying we are forced to live under men's rule. The percentage of women occupying key state roles globally is indeed so insignificant that it cannot but appear as the exception confirming the rule – of men. Across 144 states assessed in 2018, for instance, women head of states were a meagre 11 per cent, while, on average, just 18 per cent of government ministers and 24 per cent of parliamentarians were women.[7]

This means it is not an exaggeration to say that it is largely men who decide the rules according to which we live: they decide what is legal and what is illegal; who/how and when to pay taxes; who/how and when one can be employed, inherit property, have marriages, have or not have healthcare, have or not have free kindergarten, have or not have an abortion, a sex change, and so forth. Given that we live under such a menocracy, are we surprised to learn that the gender pay gap is a worldwide phenomenon and that women are paid on average 63 per cent of what men get?[8]

No, we are not surprised.

Does this mean that we should fight to have women presidents to fix things?

No, it means we should fight to have no presidents at all. There can be no feminist state because feminism means fighting against the oppression of all women,[9] and the state is, and has always been, the tool whereby a minority of people rule over the vast majority. But feminism cannot mean the liberation of just a few women. We have another name for that: elitism. As Chinese anarchafeminist He Zhen pointed out long ago, the majority of women are already oppressed both by the government and by men. The electoral system simply increases their oppression by introducing a third ruling group: elite women.[10] Even if we added a woman president and a few more women ministers, the majority of women would still be taken advantage of by men with the help of a minority of women. When a few women in power dominate the majority of powerless women, unequal class differentiation is brought into existence. If the majority of women do not want to be controlled by men, why would they want to be controlled by a minority of women? Instead of competing with men for power, He Zhen concluded, women should strive to overthrow men's rule.

The relevance of He Zhen's words, written in 1907, shows how prophetic anarchafeminism has been from its very inception. Why anarchafeminism? Because it is the best antidote against the possibility of feminism becoming simply class elitism or, even worse, white privilege. In an epoch when the election of a single woman as president is often presented as liberation for *all* women – when women such as Ivanka Trump can claim feminist battles by transforming the hashtag *#womenwhowork* into a fashion brand while forgetting that, for every elite *#womanwhoworks*, some less fortunate women will have to replace them in house and childcare – the fundamental message of anarchafeminists of the past is more urgent than ever: "Feminism does not mean female corporate power or a woman president: it means no corporate power and no president."[11]

Against the violence perpetrated by sovereign states in order to maintain the sovereign sex in its privilege, we anarchafeminists call for the liberation of all women. Not one less! Either all, or none of us will be free.

IN THE BEGINNING WAS MOVEMENT: AGAINST BOUNDARIES AS A TOOL FOR DOMINATION

Anarchism does not mean absence of order, but rather searching for a social order without an orderer.[12] The main orderer of our established ways of thinking about politics is the state, and the main tool whereby states control the population within their territories is the policing of boundaries. It is through the bureaucratic apparatus of the state that a gender identity becomes attached to us from the time we are assigned a sex at birth: from the moment birth attendants determine our "sex," it gets inscribed in our state ID, documents, and passports, and will remain with us for the rest of our lives (except for those who undergo a sex change). But why does the state need to know and monitor our sex and gender?

Furthermore, it is because we are so accustomed to living in sovereign states under the aegis of passports that we tend to perceive the migration of bodies around the globe as a problem.[13] On the contrary, we should remember that, whereas sovereign states are a relatively recent historical phenomenon (for most of humanity, people have lived under other types of political formations),[14] human beings have been migrating across Earth since the very appearance of so-called *Homo sapiens*.[15] *Homo sapiens* is thus also an *esse migrans*. Hence the need to visualize a form of feminism before and beyond boundaries.

Adopting an anarchafeminist lens means indeed taking the entire globe as the framework for considering the liberation of women. Doing so implies a critique of the state apparatus, but it also going beyond any form of methodological nationalism, that is, any way of privileging certain women and LGBTQI+ bodies and thus certain national or regional contexts. If fighting the oppression of women means we have to fight all forms of oppression, then statism and nationalism cannot be an exception. If one begins by looking at the dynamics of exploitation by taking state boundaries as an unquestionable fact, one will automatically end up reinforcing one of the very tools for gender oppression that was meant to be questioned in the first place. In the form of a slogan, we might say, "the globe first," because the framework is the message, and adopting anything less than the entire globe as our framework today is at best naïve provincialism, and at worst obnoxious ethnocentrism. Neither is beneficial for the cause of women and LGBTQI+ people.[16]

But looking at the globe without addressing the legacy of colonialism and the race system in the global production of knowledge is to risk reproducing the same patterns of oppression and silencing of marginalized voices: "Globalization without deimperialization is simply a disguised reproduction of imperialist conquest."[17] Whereas several feminist theories produced in the global North have failed to understand the extent to which the emancipation of white, middle-class women took place at the expense of a renewed oppression of working-class racialized bodies, and have often ignored the contribution of their black and brown sisters,[18] anarchafeminists are by definition called to adopt an inclusive perspective that recognizes the capacity for theory-making of all the voices fighting against oppression worldwide. For anarchafeminists, it is pivotal to bring to the centre of the discussion texts produced worldwide, thereby arguing for a form of feminism beyond racism, and beyond ethnocentrism. "For the master's tools will never dismantle the master's house."[19] And no white European master is ever going to dismantle his own house as a gesture of courtesy toward the second sex in the rest of the world. We have to bring it down ourselves.

To do so, we must take the entire globe as our framework for thinking about women's liberation. By exploring the processes of production and reproduction of life independent of state boundaries and through a plurality of voices, not only will we be able to avoid the pitfalls of any form of methodological nationalism but we will also be able to perceive the global interconnectedness of different forms of domination, beginning with the intertwining of capitalist exploitation, colonial domination, and gender discrimination. Boundaries are a tool of global menocracy because state boundaries constitute the primary administrators of space and thus the regulators of the flux of labour, capital, and the movement of bodies around the globe.

Against the violence perpetrated in the name of state boundaries and the racism they support, against the historical amnesia that leads us to forget that at the beginning was movement, we anarchafeminists call for the liberation of all women. Not one less! Either all, or none of us will be free.

CAPITAL SINS: GENDER, RACE, AND THE ENVIRONMENT

If we take the globe as our framework, the first striking datum to emerge is that people around the globe have not always been "doing" gender, and, moreover, even if they had been, it would have been on very different terms. It is only with the emergence of European colonialism through a worldwide capitalist system that the rigid gender binarism we are now accustomed to became so dominant. This does not mean that sexual difference did not exist before capitalism; nor that global capitalism invented patriarchy from scratch. It simply means that binary gender roles were not as universally accepted as the primary criteria by which to classify bodies as they are today. It was modern capitalism that made the mononuclear bourgeois family, with its binary gender roles, hegemonic, thereby giving a new and powerful driving force to premodern forms of patriarchy.

Socialist feminists have long emphasized how capitalism needs a gendered division of labour because, being predicated on the endless expansion of profit, it needs both the extraction of surplus value from waged productive labour as well as unpaid reproductive labour, which is still performed largely by gendered bodies.[20] Put bluntly, capitalism needs "women," because it needs the assumption that women are not "working" when they wash their husband's and children's socks: it needs them to believe that they are just performing their natural tasks and thus being good wives and mothers. As Cinzia Arruzza, Tithi Bhattacharya, and Nancy Fraser recently put it: "capitalist society harbors a social-reproductive contradiction: a tendency to commandeer for capital's benefit as much 'free' reproductive labor as possible, without any concern for its replenishment. As a result, it periodically gives rise to 'crises of care,' which exhaust women, ravage families, and stretch social energies to the breaking point."[21]

The perception that women's labour is not proper work, but simply the obligation of their gender, is pivotal to keeping the division between productive and reproductive work, between "waged labour," subject to exploitation, and "unwaged labour," subject to "super-exploitation."[22] This form of gendered exploitation is "super" because, whereas the exploitation of waged labour takes place through the extraction of surplus value, that of women's domestic labour takes place via a denial of the very status of work. The exploitation of women's work is therefore not only patent in phenomena such as the gender pay gap, the fact that women worldwide are generally paid less for the same job;[23] it is most evident in the fact that a great part of their daily work is not paid at all.

A lot of the reproductive work performed by women in the global South is excluded from the wage labour market, but is strictly dependent on the use of natural resources and the environment: what appear to multinational corporations as "weeds" to be eliminated are often gardens that women draw their subsistence from. Whereas the monocultures and industrial farmers produce capital for global markets, the cost of that production is often the destruction of the natural environment that provided Indigenous women with the means for subsistence. As ecofeminists have pointed out for quite some time, what industrialism sees as "nature," that is as something that is available for free, is all too often the result of the labour of the second sex.[24]

Along with the extraction of free labour from women, capitalism also needs to extract free natural resources from the environment and to create mechanisms for regulating the flux of labour. This is the reason that capitalism has from the very beginning gone hand in hand with colonialism, that is with the forced extraction of natural resources from occupied lands and the establishment of relationships of domination whereby Indigenous majorities are ruled by minorities of foreign invaders. The occupation of foreign lands by force has been the enabler for the extraction of natural resources that have never been repaid, either to nature itself or to the native inhabitants of those lands. The invention of the modern race system made it possible to regulate the world labour market by guaranteeing that slaves could be dispossessed of their lives and labour, whereas mestizos and Indigenous people could also be either completely disposed of or only minimally recompensed.[25]

By building on these insights, Maria Lugones has recently revised the thesis of a "coloniality of modern power" and put forward the very useful concept of "coloniality of gender."[26] With this term, she emphasizes how the binary division "men/women" and the classification of bodies according to their racial belonging went together, being exported by Europeans through the very process of colonial expansion that accompanied the worldwide spread of capitalism. Within the American context, she pointed out how gender roles were much more flexible and variegated before the advent of European settlement. Different Indigenous nations had, for instance, a third gender category to positively recognize intersex and queer subjectivities, whereas others, such as the Yuma, "had a tradition of gender designation based on dreams; a female [that is, one assigned female at birth] who dreamed of weapons became a male for all practical purposes."[27]

Furthermore, it is manifest, and yet all too often forgotten, that to classify people on the basis of their genitalia is not an a priori of human mind, either. Classifying bodies on the basis of their sex, as well as classifying them on the basis of their race, implies, among other things, a primacy of the visual register. Such a primacy, according to Oyèrónké Oyěwùmí, is typical of the West, particularly when looked at from the perspective of some African pre-colonial cultures such as the Yoruba. As she points out in her seminal text *The Invention of*

Women, the Yoruba cultures, for instance, relied much more on the oral transmission of information than on its visualization, and they valued age over all other criteria for social hegemony.[28] Before colonialism they did not even have a name to contrast men and women. And yet, we live now in a world where gender binarism has become ubiquitous, and where men, and in particular white men, are constantly propped up as the sovereign sex.

Against this systematic intertwining of capitalist economy, racial classification of bodies, and gender oppression – against this boundary-drawing that separates women from each other in order to make them more exploitable, we anarchafeminists call for the liberation of all women. Not one less! (*Ni una menos!*) Either all, or none of us will be free.

ANOTHER WOMAN IS POSSIBLE

Why feminism and why women? At this point one may object: why insist on the concept of feminism and not just call this anarchism? Why focus only on women? If the purpose is to dismantle all types of oppressive hierarchies, should we not also get rid of this very gender binary which opposes "women" to "men," and thus also imprisons us in a binary heteronormative and cisnormative matrix?

We respond by pointing out that when we say "women" we are not speaking about an eternal essence, or even about a predetermined object. Indeed, to articulate a specifically feminist position while maintaining a multifaceted understanding of domination, we call for a more nuanced understanding of "womanhood." Women are not objects, but processes of becoming; they are not things, but relations. By drawing insights from an ontology of the transindividual, we argue that bodies in general, and women's bodies in particular, must not be considered as individuals, as objects given once and for all, but rather as never complete processes.[29]

Women's bodies, like all bodies, are bodies in plural because they are processes, processes constituted by mechanisms of affects and associations that occur at the *inter-*, *intra-* and *supra*-individual level. While bodies come into being through an *inter*-individual encounter, such as that of a sperm and an ovum, they are shaped by *supra*-individual forces such as their geographical locations, and are made up by *intra*-individual bodies, such as the air we breathe or the hormones we absorb. Every molecule that we inhale and every atom that we eat, not to mention the millions of bacteria and other individuals inhabiting our bodies, is part of our transindividual being.

Notice here the benefits of using such an ontological shift toward transindividuality as the prism through which women's individuality must be understood. First, instead of elaborating a form of feminism and then having to add ecology as something different from feminism itself, here the two positions are unified from the start because, in an ontology of the transindividual, the environment is not something separate from us, but rather, the environment is us – literally something constitutive of our individuality. A form of anarchafeminism rooted in an ontology of the transindividual is therefore also by definition a form of eco-feminism in which all animate and inanimate bodies, not simply human forms of life, are potentially involved. Second, imaginal collective formations such as sex, race, and class are from the outset conceptualized as constitutive of our individuality, and thus as intimately intertwined. Third, when women's bodies are theorized as transindividual processes, we can speak about "women" without incurring the charge of essentialism or culturalism. There is no place here for the opposition between sex (nature) and gender (culture) because there is no place for body-mind dualism, since every body, animate or inanimate, is constitutive of our being.

To sum up on this point, by adopting a transindividual ontology, we can also use the concept of woman beyond a cis-normative or hetero-normative framework, and thus include all types of women: feminine women, masculine women, women assigned female or male at birth, bisexual women, trans women, cis women, asexual women, queer women, and so forth. Only if women's bodies are theorized as processes, as sites of a process of becoming that takes place at different levels, only then will we be able to speak about "women" without falling into hetero- or cis-normativity. If we adopt this transindividual ontology, we can also use the concept of woman in such a way that it comes to include all those bodies that identify themselves and are identified through the always changing narrative of "womanhood."

In other words, a transindividual understanding such as this allows us to articulate the question, "What does it mean to be a woman?" in pluralistic terms, while also defending a specifically feminist form of anarchism. Although the concept of transindividuality does not mean transgender, we believe that by understanding bodies as the results of transindividual processes of becoming also helps to invert the overall general perspective and fight transphobia at its very source:

within this ontological framework, far from being a deviation from the norm, the process of transforming and transgendering immediately appears as one of the possible expressions of our transindividual nature, and not as an exception from it. To put it bluntly, we could say that such a transindividual ontology points to the fact that another woman is not just possible: it has also, and always, already begun.

Against the violence perpetrated in the name of gender binarism, homophobia, and transphobia, we anarchafeminists call for the liberation of all women. Not one less! Either all, or none of us will be free.

NOTES

1 These are the data provided by the United Nations Population Fund, but statistics vary widely as it is an obviously difficult phenomenon to track. Unfpa.org., "Gender-Biased Sex Selection," *United Nations Population Fund*, 2020, https://www.unfpa.org/gender-biased-sex-selection. The Charlotte Lozier Institute gives an ever-more-alarming number of 160 million "missing girls." See Anna Higgins, "Sex-Selection Abortion: The Real War on Women," *Charlotte Lozier Institute*, 13 April 2016, https://lozierinstitute.org/sex-selection-abortion-the-real-war-on-women/.

2 Unwomen.org, "Facts and Figures: Ending Violence against Women," UN Women, 2019, https://www.unwomen.org/en/what-we-do/ending-violence-against-women/facts-and-figures.

3 Liz Ford, "'Calamitous': Domestic Violence Set to Soar by 20% during Global Lockdown," *The Guardian*, 28 April 2020, https://www.theguardian.com/global-development/2020/apr/28/calamitous-domestic-violence-set-to-soar-by-20-during-global-lockdown-coronavirus.

4 I use the term "first sex" to indicate that, in comparison to men, women and LGTQB+ people occupy the position of a "second sex." The implicit reference is the fortunate title of de Beauvoir's masterpiece, which remains unfortunately quite timely as women are still largely the second sex to men. I am, however, here unifying both women and LGTQB+ folks in the category of "second sex" to mean that we are both excluded from the "first sex." Simone de Beauvoir, *The Second Sex,* trans. Constance Borde and Sheila Malovany-Chevallier (New York: Alfred A. Knopf, 2010).

5 Hillary Lazar, "Until All Are Free: Black Feminism, Anarchism, and Interlocking Oppression," *Perspectives on Anarchist Theory*, no. 29 (2016): 35–50.

6 Political theorists have been pointing to this nature of the modern state for quite some time. Within the West, this was clearly articulated by Jean-Jacques Rousseau, for instance, when he wrote: "If we follow the progress of inequality through these different revolutions, we will find that the establishment of the Law and Right of property was its first term; the institution of Magistracy, the second; the conversion of legitimate into arbitrary power the third and last; so that the state of rich and poor was authorized by the first Epoch, that of powerful and weak by the second, and by the third that of Master and Slave, which is the last degree of inequality, and the state to which all the others finally lead, until new revolutions either dissolve the Government entirely, or bring it closer to legitimate institution." See Jean-Jacques Rousseau, *The Discourses and Other Early Political Writings*, ed. and trans. Victor Gourevitch (Cambridge: Cambridge University Press, 1997), 182. Marx and Engels's critique of the state as the tool whereby the bourgeoisie has "agglomerated population, centralized means of production, and ... concentrated property in a few hands" is reminiscent of Rousseau's critique. See Karl Marx and Friedrich Engels, *The Communist Manifesto*, trans. Samuel Moore (London: Verso, 1998), 35, 40. Finally, whereas Marxists considered it at times possible to use the state apparatus through a dictatorship of the proletariat aimed at a communist revolution, anarchist theorists from Mikhail Bakunin to Emma Goldman were relentless in their critique. As Bakunin wrote, when contesting the idea of a dictatorship of the proletariat: "The only difference between revolutionary dictatorship and the state is in external appearances. Essentially, they both represent the same government of the majority by a minority in the name of the presumed stupidity of the one and the presumed intelligence of the other. Therefore they are equally reactionary, both having the direct and inevitable result of consolidating the political and economic privileges of the governing minority and the political and economic slavery of the masses." Mikhail Bakunin, *Statism and Anarchy*, trans. Marshall S. Shatz (Cambridge: Cambridge University Press, 2005), 137.

7 World Economic Forum, "Global Gender Gap Report 2018," *World Economic Forum*, 2018, http://reports.weforum.org/global-gender-gap-report-2018/key-findings/?doing_wp_cron=1558904216.84949302673 33984375000.

8 See footnote 5 and Rupert Neate, "Global Pay Gap Will Take 202 Years to Close, says World Economic Forum," *The Guardian*, 18 December 2018,

https://www.theguardian.com/world/2018/dec/18/global-gender-pay-gap-will-take-202-years-to-close-says-world-economic-forum.

9 Bell Hooks, *Feminist Theory: from Margin to Center* (London: Pluto, 2000).

10 He Zhen, "Women's Liberation," in *Anarchism: A Documentary History of Libertarian Ideas,* ed. Robert Graham, (Montreal: Black Rose Books, 2005), 341.

11 Peggy Kornegger, "Anarchism: The Feminist Connection," in *Quiet Rumors* (Oakland: AK Press, 2012), 25.

12 Chiara Bottici, "Anarchy," in *The Encyclopedia of Political Science Vol. 1,* ed. George Thomas Kurian (Washington, DC: CQ Press, 2011), 52–4.

13 "Historical evidence indicates clearly that, well into the nineteenth century, people routinely regarded as 'foreign' those from the next province every bit as much as those who came from other 'countries.'" John Torpey, *The Invention of the Passport: Surveillance, Citizenship and the State,* 2nd ed. (Cambridge: Cambridge University Press, 2018), 11–12.

14 See Gianfranco Poggi, *The Development of the Modern State,* particularly chapter 5, in which the term "modern state" is specifically located within the nineteenth century. Gianfranco Poggi, *The Development of the Modern State: A Sociological Introduction* (Stanford: Stanford University Press, 1978).

15 As Peter Bellwood argued, by combing the records of biology, archaeology, and comparative linguistics, we find evidence of perpetual migration from "the initial migrations of the incipient genus *Homo,* around two million years ago, to the relatively recent but still prehistoric migrations of populations such as the Eastern Polynesians and Thule Inuit." Peter Bellwood, "Introduction," in *The Global Prehistory of Human Migration,* ed. Peter Bellwood (Chichester: John Wiley & Sons, 2015), 1–6.

16 It has been shown, for instance, how the narrative that "we need to protect our women from those brown men" has only been reinforcing a form of femonationalism that did not bring any good to women's cause. See Sara R. Farris, *In the Name of Women's Rights: The Rise of Femonationalism* (Durham: Duke University Press, 2017).

17 Kuan-Hsing Chen, "Globalization and Deimperialization," in *Asia as Method: Toward Deimperialism* (Durham: Duke University Press, 2010), 2.

18 Audre Lorde, *The Master's Tools Will Never Dismantle the Master's House* (London: Penguin, 2017), 16–21.

19 Ibid., 19.

20 Kathi Weeks, *The Problem with Work: Feminism, Marxism, Antiwork Politics, and Postwork Imaginaries* (Durham: Duke University Press, 2011). Among other texts on Marxist feminism see Silvia Federici, *Revolution at Point Zero: Housework, Reproduction, and Feminist Struggle* (Oakland: PM Press, 2012); and the useful edited volume Shahrzad Mojab, *Marxism and Feminism* (London: Zed Books, 2015). For a recent account of marxist feminism in the form of a manifesto, see Cinzia Arruzza, Tithi Bhattacharya, and Nancy Fraser, *Feminism for the 99%* (New York: Verso, 2019), 65.

21 Arruzza, Bhattacharya, and Fraser, *Feminism for the 99%*, 65.

22 Marie Mies, *Patriarchy and Accumulation on a World Scale: Women in the International Division of Labour* (London: Zed Books, 1986).

23 Neate, "Global Pay Gap Will Take 202 Years to Close."

24 Marie Mies and Vandana Shiva, *Ecofeminism* (London: Zed Books, 2014).

25 As Anibal Quijano observes: "In the Hispanic region, the Crown of Castilla decided early on to end the enslavement of the Indians in order to prevent their total extermination. They were instead confined to serfdom. For those that lived in communities, the ancient practice of reciprocity – the exchange of labour force and labour without a market – was allowed as a way of reproducing its labour force as serfs. In some cases, the Indian nobility, a reduced minority, were exempt from serfdom and received special treatment owing to their roles as intermediaries with the dominant race. They were also permitted to participate in some of the activities of the non-noble Spanish. However, Blacks were reduced to slavery. As the dominant race, Spanish and Portuguese whites could receive wages, be independent merchants, independent artisans, or independent farmers – in short, independent producers of commodities. Nevertheless, only nobles could participate in the high-to-midrange positions in the military and civil colonial administration." Following these insights, it does not appear as an exaggeration to say that races largely worked as job descriptions. Anibal Quijano and Michael Ennis, "Coloniality of Power, Eurocentrism, and Latin America," *Nepantla: Views from the South* 1, no. 3 (2000): 553.

26 Maria Lugones, "The Coloniality of Gender," in *The Palgrave Handbook of Gender and Development: Critical Engagements in Feminist Theory and Practice*, ed. Wendy Harcourt (New York: Palgrave Macmillan, 2016).

27 Ibid., 25.

28 Oyèrónké Oyěwùmí, *The Invention of Women: Making an African Sense of Western Gender Discourses* (Minneapolis: University of Minnesota Press, 1997).

29 "The term 'woman' becomes … the shortcut for a story that keeps together a series of processes and potentialities that we can associate with individuals instituted as and instituting themselves as 'women.'" Chiara Bottici, "Bodies in Plural: Towards an Anarcha-Feminist Manifesto," *Thesis Eleven* 142, no. 1 (2017): 100.

13

Rebellious Mothering:
Gendered Labour of Revolutionary Acts in the Time of COVID

Jennifer D. Grubbs

In March of 2020 I received a text message that a good friend of mine had been admitted to the Intensive Care Unit (ICU). She had been having trouble breathing and thought she might have contracted the novel coronavirus. While she awaited her COVID-19 test results, she went into cardiac arrest. In a video she later shared with family and friends, she explained the gasping, the sense of drowning, and the vulnerability she felt while she was alone, dying in the ICU. Overcome with fear, she stressed that one specific question frightened her the most: would her youngest child remember her if she died?

The global health pandemic has placed great emphasis on breath: masking our droplets, measuring the distance between ourselves and the breath of others, and monitoring our pulse oxygen level. The virus wreaks havoc on the human body, and in particular, on the respiratory system. We, the global "we," are given the immense and insurmountable task of containing the air which we exhale. Nearly two months after my friend was brought back to life with medically assisted breathing devices, another Black man was murdered by the deprivation of oxygen.

A store clerk had called the police to report that a customer (allegedly George Floyd) had used a counterfeit $20. Shortly thereafter, police officers approached Floyd in his vehicle. The very first words from Floyd that appear in the police transcripts of their exchange are, "Hey, man. I'm sorry!" quickly followed by, "I'm sorry, I'm sorry!"[1] As the officers yell for him to put his "fucking" hands where they can be seen, Floyd pleads for confirmation that they will not shoot him. He directly asks officer Thomas Lane: "Mr Officer, please don't shoot me. Please, man ... I'll look at you eye-to-eye, man. Please don't shoot me, man ... Please don't shoot me, Mr Officer. Please, don't shoot me, man. Please. Can you not shoot me, man?"[2] Throughout the exchange, Floyd begs not to be shot and reasserts that he will cooperate.

The officers note that Floyd's body language is "squirrely," and they invoke the racist assumption that he is intoxicated and aggressive. At one point, Floyd clarifies directly why he is acting erratic: "I'm scared, man." Not only is Floyd fearful of being shot, but he vocalizes a fear of being left alone in small spaces. He continues to ask the officers for compassion and begs them to let him sit outside for questioning. After a series of pleas, and a blatant disregard from officers Lane and J. Alexander Kueng, Floyd begins to experience trouble breathing.

He screams, "I can't breathe," while officer Derek Chauvin places his knee firmly on Floyd's neck. He asserts over and over, at least twenty times during the nearly nine-minute video, "I can't breathe," and begs for just an ounce of the humanity awarded to those with white-skin privilege in the United States. As Floyd struggles to breathe, he continues to cry out in desperation. With Chauvin's knee slowly suffocating him, Floyd cries, "Mom, I love you. Tell my kids I love them. I'm dead." The last words we hear on the audio, and which appear in the police transcript, are, "Ah! Ah! Please. Please. Please."[3] As Floyd gasps for air, he shouts for his "mama" nearly a dozen times. While he struggles to catch his breath, he bellows out, "They going to kill me. They're going to kill me, man." As officer Chauvin presses his knee even more firmly into Floyd's neck, he callously replies, "Takes a heck of a lot of oxygen to say that."[4]

The death of Floyd, particularly the method of police brutality (suffocation), tapped into the collective trauma of the 2014 murder of Eric Garner. The repeated onslaught of state-sanctioned violence against Black men in the United States demands a public reckoning. While COVID surged across the country and economic instability was exacerbated by shelter-in-place mandates, people were summoned to the streets to protest Floyd's murder. Mothers already overburdened with work (both paid and unpaid) found themselves outraged by the unanswered cries of George Floyd. The spatialization of white supremacy in America is codified in these cries.

But its powerful call out to humanity was the accumulation of the cries of hundreds of years of violation and suffering, and resisting and surviving. In so doing, it snagged the veil that covers the U.S. claim of a just and fair modern democratic order. It re-surfaced and re-exposed America's long fractured society that dwells within its nationalistic perimeters. Hence, today, Floyd's last words "I can't breathe" serve as a reminder of the hypocrisy that shrouds the long-standing aura around Washington, D.C., which has always stolen its way toward an "ideal democratic landscape" and, also paradoxically, never ceases to be the signature and epitome of colonial power. D.C.'s beautiful landscape was a design tool that has long served to bury and obscure the nation's Black history. It has existed as a glittering codification of White supremacy and fragile hegemony.[5]

The compounding occurrence of police murders and COVID-19 provided fertile ground to take on these deeply rooted social structures.

The week that Floyd died, there were 209 identified deaths in Minnesota from COVID-19.[6] In the state, over 850,000 public school children remained at home instead of going to school, because of state-mandated closures.[7] Businesses across the state closed their doors, many never to open them again. Despite the public health risks, people gathered *en masse* to demand some semblance of justice. Countrywide, existing campaigns that focused on defunding, examining, and holding the police accountable gained traction. In hundreds of cities across the country, with global solidarity actions around the world, people took to the streets in protest. They demanded justice for Trayvon Martin, Tanisha Anderson, Michael Brown, Tamir Rice, Gabriella Nevarez, Akai Gurley, Eric Garner, Samuel DuBose, Janisha Fonville, Walter Scott, Freddie Gray, Michelle Cusseaux, Alton Sterling, Philando Castile, Elijah McClain, Botham Jean, Stephen Clark, Aura Rosser, Atatiana Jefferson, Breonna Taylor, George Floyd, Daniel Prude, Rayshard Brooks, Justine Diamond, Tony Timpa, and so many more.[8]

These culminating moments after Floyd's death, referred to as the George Floyd uprisings, invoked the memory and pain of each Black person brutalized and murdered by law enforcement. In some ways, this period was stabilized by the *de*stabilization of the global health pandemic. Government ineptitude in the United States left millions of people without adequate personal protective equipment, shuttered businesses and academic institutions, and overburdened the underprepared healthcare systems. Public discourse focused on the structural failings of the Trump administration, and it amplified the overarching structural failings of the United States as a whole.

The country reached a state of rupture:

> With millions of American families facing an uncertain start to the school year, the struggle for child care, education and economic stability is fueling a political uprising, built on the anger of women who find themselves constantly – and indefinitely – expected to be teacher, caregiver, employee and parent ...
> Women were more likely than men to report having participated in protests over the past two years, and mothers with children in the home were twice as likely as fathers to report participating in a protest, according to a Kaiser Family Foundation poll from June.[9]

The George Floyd protests were indicative of much larger structural critiques that had been buried under generations of white supremacy and rugged individualism. With everything around them closed, white mothers were brought to a halt and bombarded with the overwhelming reality of racialized police violence. And as they watched and listened to the audio, Floyd summoned not just his own mother, but all mothers.

In a global context, mothers have held prominent spaces within political organizing. From Cuba to Mexico to Iran, mothers have successfully challenged oppressive regimes. Through strategic essentialism, boycotts, and nonviolent resistance, mothers have taken on a multitude of issues. But this engagement has not been without its challenges. Within the United States, feminist movements are steeped in, informed by, and entangled with systemic racism. White mothers have consistently situated themselves in positions of authority in relation to Black mothers and prioritized their own demands for humanity. Mikki Kendall explains:

> Too often white women decide that when they feel uncomfortable, upset, or threatened, they can turn to the patriarchy for protection. Because they don't want to lose that protection (dubious as it is), they stand by when it's convenient, and challenge it only when it directly threatens them. Yet, they know they benefit from it being challenged, and thus rely on others to do the heaviest lifting. They fail to recognize the conflicted relationship they have

with the patriarchy includes a certain cowardice around challenging not only it, but other women who have embraced it.[10]

The women's suffrage movement, for example, relied on the racist politics of respectability even if it meant leaving Black women behind.[11] Issues of equity are constantly stratified along racial lines, allowing white mothers to define themselves by what they are not: Black mothers.

In Portland, under the fascistic rhetoric of Trump, federal agents were deployed to suppress and intimidate protestors. A group of people who identified as mothers, organized by Beverly Barnum, decided to leverage their privilege as white and form human walls that would protect and shield protestors.[12] The groups became known as the Wall of Moms across the country. Barnum had posted a call in a local Working Moms Facebook group, asking mothers to show up at the vigil for Shai'India Harris (an eighteen-year-old woman who had been murdered that summer). Pockets of white mothers, particularly those residing in the suburbs, came to the vigil to serve as a human barricade between the federal agents and demonstrators. Across the country, mothers began organizing their own "walls" at local demonstrations. As the tactic rose to prominence, so too did the critiques.

The revolutionary act of showing up, using their bodies as strategic capital to protect demonstrators, became intertwined with hegemonic privilege. The white-saviourism that the Wall of Moms invoked, coupled with the centring of white women's bodies within a movement focused on the brutalized Black body, was inescapably problematic. The protests and vigils were overtaken by a sea of white women in yellow clothing singing "Hands up, don't shoot!" lullabies. Black mothers, the mothers actually summoned by their babies being brutalized by the carceral system, were decentred.

I watched much of this unfold while sheltering in place, juggling professional commitments and insurmountable domestic tasks as a mother of four young children. I felt summoned, but I was not sure by whom or to what I felt summoned. Public protest has always felt like an appropriate mechanism for me to externalize my rage against the systems. I have chanted, "Whose Streets?" "Our Streets," hundreds of times at countless demonstrations. And although the performative power of reclaiming the streets has served as a vital coping mechanism, the spatialization of public spaces can be hijacked.[13] This moment felt fundamentally different. These streets were not mine; these streets should not be mine at this particular moment. The streets had been paved by white supremacy, and if they are to be reclaimed, it should not be by more white bodies.

After my children's school closed in mid-March 2020, I became their one-stop shop for companionship, entertainment, education, mental health support, food inventory management, meal planning and prepping, public health data interpretation, masking information ... the list goes on. Without external childcare, my partner and I took turns serving in these various roles. Despite our best efforts, I inevitably assumed a disproportionate number of roles and responsibilities. I took on these roles, referred to as gendered labour, in addition to the increased professional demands I assumed when the college I teach at pivoted to remote learning. While our home became a dumpster fire of multi-tasking, the George Floyd uprisings continued to grow. I reflected on how my Jewish ancestors, my own rebellious mothers, had resisted oppressive regimes in Nazi-occupied Poland. I wondered what modes of everyday resistance I could incorporate that named, challenged, and undermined white supremacy.

As a mother raising four white children, two of whom are gendered male, I am tasked with the privileged burden of undoing the foundation of the house that, although I did not build it, I inhabit. How, then, can we begin to rearticulate our gendered labour as revolutionary acts? During this lengthy time of dormancy, I have carved out intentional space to discuss with my children how whiteness functions. We said their names and told their stories. We attended outdoor, socially distanced listening sessions and smaller protests that connected local racial injustices. On one sunny afternoon, we decided to let the kids play on the playground after a demonstration. The humidity had finally broken, and it was one of the first days in weeks that you could stand outside without immediately perspiring.

The kids, with their masks tightly hugging the bridge of their nose and curving all the way underneath their chin, had gravitated toward the playground nearby. I walked toward the fenced-in area with one of the organizers, a Black woman. Her son was roughly the same age as our child, and they appeared to get along. After ten minutes or so, the boys started arguing over a stick they had found. This was not just any stick; it had branches jutting out each side and infinite imaginary potential. My four-year-old began teasing the other child and reciting the colonial adage, "Finders keepers." I explained that the stick doesn't belong to anyone and encouraged him to play with something else. He refused and continued to argue over the stick. Following a stubborn exchange, my son agreed to let the other boy have it.

After the boys had run off and resumed their game, I stood next to the mother and began apologizing for my son. She said she felt bad that my child had to give up the stick and insisted that her son needed to work on sharing. I reasserted that my child also needed to work on sharing, and that he had been wrong to taunt her child when he was down. We laughed it off as children being children and began talking about something else. Later that night, I reflected on the encounter. I pictured my son and the boy on the playground redistributing a material resource (the stick) after a brief conflict. I remembered how they played that afternoon, gasping for air from laughter and running. What would this exchange look like between our children in a different context? In ten years? The stick on the playground started to feel like a metaphor for the present-day reckoning with white supremacy. I wondered what made it possible for our children to transform their anger and vulnerability into humility and joy. My white son was told that his turn with the stick was over, and that it was time to pass it on to the other child who happened to be Black. And, despite his initial resistance, he did.

I was brought back to the video of Floyd's murder, and the exchange between the officers while he lay unconscious. One of the officers asked Lane if he was all right, and he replied, "My knee might be a little scratched, but I'll survive." The officers shrugged at the inconvenience and disregarded the precious human life being crushed under their knee. The man who had begged for compassion minutes earlier, on the other hand, would not survive. If we are to believe that there is a sort of banality to the evil that surrounds us, then how can we engage in revolutionary acts of care that will counter it?

As we wrap our faces in masks, measure the distance between our bodies and those we encounter, and quantify the number of minutes we spend in closed spaces with others, how do we create intimate, vulnerable space together? I was not summoned by Floyd that May afternoon. I was summoned by Chauvin and Lane, and the white bystanders who refuse to see value in the life of Black men. At a minimum, I am summoned by my own children, summoned to do the work that is necessary to unravel white supremacy from the geopolitical DNA of this country. At best, my feminist politics will continue to inform my rebellious mothering while I attempt to survive a global health pandemic. Despite the suffocating nature of the gendered labour and uncertainty, I cannot take for granted the privilege it is to breathe.

NOTES

1 Minnesota District Court, "George Floyd Transcript" (2020).
2 Ibid.
3 Ibid.
4 Ibid.
5 Samayeen Nubras, Adrian Wong, and Cameron McCarthy, "Space to Breathe: George Floyd, BLM Plaza and the Monumentalization of Divided American Urban Landscapes," *Educational Philosophy and Theory*, 23 July 2020: 1–11, https://doi.org/10.1080/00131857.2020.1795980.
6 "Provisional Death Counts for Coronavirus Disease 2019 (COVID-19)," 1 February 2021, https://www.cdc.gov/nchs/nvss/vsrr/covid19/index.html.
7 "Map: Where Are Schools Closed," 28 July 2020, https://www.edweek.org/leadership/map-where-are-schools-closed/2020/07.
8 Alia Chugtai, "Know Their Names: Black People Killed by the Police in the US," *Al Jazeera*, 9 June 2020, https://interactive.aljazeera.com/aje/2020/know-their-names/index.html.
9 Lisa Lerer and Jennifer Medina, "The 'Rage Moms' Democrats Are Counting On," *The New York Times*, 17 August 2020, https://www.nytimes.com/2020/08/17/us/politics/democrats-women-voters-anger.html.
10 Mikki Kendall, *Hood Feminism: Notes from the Women That a Movement Forgot* (New York: Viking, 2020), 166.
11 bell hooks, *Ain't I a Woman? Black Women and Feminism* (New York: Routledge, 2015); Brittney C. Cooper, *Beyond Respectability: The Intellectual Thought of Race Women* (Urbana; Chicago; Springfield: University of Illinois Press, 2017).
12 Jogger Blaec, "The Complicated Rise and Swift Fall of Portland's Wall of Moms Protest Group," *Portland Monthly*, 3 August 2020, https://www.pdxmonthly.com/news-and-city-life/2020/08/the-complicated-rise-and-swift-fall-of-portland-s-wall-of-moms-protest-group.
13 Nubras, Wong, and McCarthy, "Space to Breathe."

14

The "Great Reset"? Yes, Please – But a Real One!

Slavoj Žižek

Back in April 2020, reacting to the COVID-19 outbreak, Jürgen Habermas pointed out that "Existential uncertainty is now spreading globally and simultaneously, in the heads of medially-wired individuals themselves." Furthermore, he added, "there never was so much knowing about our not-knowing and about the constraint to act and live in uncertainty."[1]

He was right to claim that this not-knowing concerns not only the pandemic itself – we at least have experts there – but even more so its economic, social, and psychic consequences. Note his precise formulation: it is not simply that we don't know what goes on, we *know* that we don't know, and this not-knowing is itself a social fact, inscribed into the way our institutions act. We now know that in, say, medieval times or early modernity they knew much less – but they didn't know this because they relied on some stable ideological foundation that guaranteed that our universe was a meaningful totality. The same holds true for some visions of communism, even for Fukuyama's idea of the end of history – they all assumed to know where history was moving.

Habermas was also right to locate the uncertainty in "the heads of medially-wired individuals": our link to the wired universe expands our knowledge tremendously, but at the same time it throws us into radical uncertainty (Are we hacked? Who controls our access? Is what we read fake news?). Ongoing discoveries about a foreign (Russian?) hacking of US government institutions and big companies exemplify this uncertainty: Americans are now discovering that they cannot even determine the methods or scope of the ongoing hacking.

The irony is that the "virus" now strikes in both meanings of the term, biological and digital.

When we try to guess what our societies will look like after the pandemic is over, the trap to avoid is futurology – futurology by definition ignores our not-knowing. Futurology can be defined as a systematic forecasting of the future on the basis of present trends in society – and therein lies the problem: futurology mostly extrapolates what will come from the present tendencies. However, what futurology doesn't take into account are historical "miracles," radical breaks that can only be explained retroactively, once they have happened. Here we should perhaps mobilize the distinction in French between *futur* and *avenir*: "*le futur*" is whatever will come after the present while "*l'avenir*" points toward a radical change. When a president wins re-election, he is "the present and future president," but he is not the president "to come" – the president to come is a different president. So, will the post-corona universe be just another future or something new "to come"?

It depends not only on science but on our political decisions. Now the time has come to say that we should have no illusions about the "happy" outcome of the US elections which brought such a relief among liberals all around the world. John Carpenter's *They Live* (1988), one of the neglected masterpieces of the Hollywood Left, tells the story of John Nada (Spanish for "nothing"), a homeless labourer who accidentally stumbles upon a pile of boxes full of sunglasses in an abandoned church. When he puts on a pair of these glasses while walking on a street, he notices that a colourful publicity billboard soliciting us to enjoy chocolate bars now simply displays the word "OBEY," while another billboard with a glamorous couple in a tight embrace, seen through the glasses, orders the viewer to "MARRY AND REPRODUCE." He also sees that paper money bears the words "THIS IS YOUR GOD." What's more, he soon discovers that many people who look charming are actually monstrous aliens with metal heads. What circulates now on the web is an image that restages a scene from *They Live* in relation to President Biden and Vice-President Harris: seen directly, the image shows the two of them smiling with the message "TIME TO HEAL"; seen through the glasses, they are two alien monsters and the message is "TIME TO HEEL."

This is, of course, part of the Trump propaganda to discredit Biden and Harris as masks of anonymous corporate machines that control our lives – but there is (more than) a grain of truth in it. Biden's victory means "future" as the continuation of the pre-Trump "normality" – that's why there was such a sigh of relief after his victory. But this "normality" means the rule of anonymous global capital, which is the true alien in our midst. I remember from my youth the desire for "Socialism with a human face" against "bureaucratic" socialism of the USSR type – Biden now promises global capitalism with a human face, but behind the face the same reality will remain. In education, this "human face" assumed the form of our obsession with "well-being": pupils and students should live in bubbles that will save them from the horrors of external reality, protected by rules of political correctness. Education is no longer intended to have a sobering effect of allowing us to confront social reality – and when we are told that this safety will prevent mental breakdowns, we should counter it with exactly the opposite claim: such false safety opens us up to mental crises when we have to confront our social reality. What "well-being activity" does is that it merely provides a false "human face" to our reality instead of enabling us to change this reality itself. Biden is the ultimate well-being president.

So why is Biden still preferable to Trump? Critics point out that Biden also lies and represents big capital, only in a more polite form; but, unfortunately, this form matters. Trump, with his vulgarization of public speech, was corroding the ethical substance of our lives (what Hegel called *Sitten*, as opposed to individual morality). This vulgarization is a worldwide process: here is a European example. Szilard Demeter, a ministerial commissioner and head of the Petofi Literary Museum in Budapest, wrote in an op-ed in November 2020: "Europe is George Soros' gas chamber. Poison gas flows from the capsule of a multicultural open society, which is deadly to the European way of life."[2] Demeter went on to characterize Soros *as* "the liberal Fuhrer," *insisting that his* "liber-aryan army deifies him more than did Hitler's own." If asked, Demeter would probably dismiss these statements as rhetorical exaggeration; this, however, would in no way dismiss their terrifying implications. The comparison between Soros and Hitler is deeply anti-Semitic: it puts Soros on a level with Hitler, claiming that the multicultural open society promoted by Soros is not only as perilous as the Holocaust and the Aryan racism that sustained it ("liber-aryan") but even worse, more perilous to the "European way of life."

So is there an alternative to this terrifying vision, other than Biden's "human face"? Greta Thunberg recently put forward three positive lessons of the pandemic: "It is possible to treat a crisis like a crisis, it is possible to put people's health above economic interests, and it is possible to listen to the science."[3] Yes, but these are possibilities. It is also possible to treat a crisis in such a way that one uses it to obfuscate other crises (like: because of the pandemic we should forget about global warming); it is also possible to use the crisis to make the rich richer and the poor poorer (which effectively happened in 2020 with unprecedented speed); and it is also possible to ignore or compartmentalize science (just recall those who refuse to take vaccines, the explosive rise of conspiracy theories, and so on). Scott Galloway gives a more or less accurate image of things in our corona time:

> We are barrelling towards a nation with three million lords being served by 350 million serfs. We don't like to say this out loud, but I feel as if this pandemic has largely been invented for taking the top 10% into the top 1%, and taking the rest of the 90% downward. We've decided to protect corporations, not people. Capitalism is literally collapsing on itself unless it rebuilds that pillar of empathy. We've decided that capitalism means being loving and empathetic to corporations, and Darwinist and harsh towards individuals.

So, which is Galloway's way out? How should we prevent social collapse? His answer is that "capitalism will collapse on itself without more empathy and love":

> We're entering the Great Reset, and it's happening quickly. Many companies will tragically be lost to the economic fallout of the pandemic, and those that do survive will exist in a different form. Organizations will be far more adaptable and resilient. Distributed teams currently thriving with less oversight will crave that same autonomy going forward. Employees will expect executives to continue leading with transparency, authenticity, and humanity.[4]

But, again, how will this be done? Galloway proposes creative destruction that lets failing business fail while protecting people who lose jobs: "*We* let people get fired so that Apple can emerge and put Sun Microsystems out of business, and then *we* take that incredible prosperity and we're more empathetic with people."[5]

The real question is, of course, who are the mysterious "we" in the last quoted sentence? How, exactly, is the redistribution to be done? Do we just tax the winners (Apple, in this case) more while allowing them to maintain their monopolist position? Galloway's idea has a certain dialectical flair: the only way to reduce inequality and poverty is to allow the market competition to do its cruel job (we let people get fired), and then … what? Do we expect market mechanisms themselves to create new jobs? Or the state? How are "love" and "empathy" operationalized? Or do we count on the winners' empathy and expect they will all behave like Bill Gates and Warren Buffett? I find this proposed supplementation of market mechanisms by morality, love, and empathy utterly problematic: instead of enabling us to get the best of both worlds (market egotism and moral empathy), it is much more probable that we'll get the worst of both worlds.

The human face of this "leading with transparency, authenticity, and humanity" consists of Gates, Jeff Bezos, and Mark Zuckerberg, the faces of authoritarian corporate capitalism, all of whom pose as humanitarian heroes, as our new aristocracy celebrated in our media and quoted as wise humanitarians. Gates gives billions to charities, but we should remember how he opposed Elisabeth Warren's plan for a small rise in taxes. He praised Thomas Piketty and once almost proclaimed himself a socialist – true, but in a very specific twisted sense: his wealth comes from privatizing what Marx called our "commons," our shared social space in which we move and communicate. Gates's wealth has nothing to do with the production costs of the products Microsoft is selling (one can even argue that Microsoft is paying its intellectual workers a relatively high salary); that is, Gates's wealth is not the result of his success in producing good software for lower prices than his competitors, or in greater "exploitation" of his hired intellectual workers. Gates became one of the richest men in the world by appropriating the rent for allowing millions of us to communicate through the medium that he privatized and controls. And in the same way that Microsoft privatized the software most of us use, personal contacts are privatized by Facebook, book purchases by Amazon, research by Google, and so forth.

There is thus a grain of truth in Trump's "rebellion" against digital corporate powers. It is worth watching the *War Room* podcasts of Steve Bannon, the greatest ideologist of Trump's populism: one cannot but be fascinated by how many partial truths he combines into an overall lie. Yes, under Obama the gap that separates wealthy from poor grew immensely, and big corporations grew stronger. But under Trump this process just carried on, continued by Trump lowering taxes and printing money mostly to save big companies, among other manoeuvres. We are thus facing a horrible false alternative: a big corporate reset or nationalist populism that turns out to make no real change. "The great reset" is the formula of how to change some things (even many things) so that things will basically remain the same.

So is there a third way, outside the space of the two extremes of restoring the old normality and a Great Reset? Yes – a true great reset. It is no secret what needs to be done – Thunberg made it clear. First, we must finally recognize the pandemic crisis for what it is, part of a global crisis of our entire way of life, from ecology to new social tensions. Second, we should establish social control and regulation over the economy. Third, we should rely on science – rely on but not simply accept it as the agency that makes decisions. Why not? Let's return to Habermas, with whom we began: our predicament is that we are compelled to act while we know we don't know the full coordinates of the situation we are in, and non-acting would itself function as an act.

But is this not the basic situation of every acting? Our great advantage is that we *know* how much we don't know, and this knowing about our not-knowing opens up the space of freedom. We act when we don't know the whole situation, but this is not simply our limitation: what gives us freedom is that the situation – in our social sphere, at least – is in itself open, not fully (pre)determined. And our situation in the pandemic is certainly open. We've learned the first lesson now: "shutdown light" is not enough. They tell us "we" (our economy) cannot afford another hard lockdown – so let's change the economy. Lockdown is the most radical negative gesture *within* the existing order. The way beyond, to a new positive order, leads through politics, not science. What we need to do is to change our economic life so that it can survive the lockdowns and emergencies that are for sure awaiting us, in the same way that a war compels us to ignore market limitations and find a way to do what is "impossible" in a free-market economy.

Back in March 2003, Donald Rumsfeld, then the US secretary of defence, engaged in a little bit of amateur philosophizing about the relationship between the known and the unknown: "There are known knowns. These are things we know that we know. There are known unknowns. That is to say, there are things that we know we don't know. But there are also unknown unknowns. There are things we don't know we don't know."[6] What he forgot to add was the crucial fourth term: the "unknown knowns" – things we don't know that we know – which is precisely the Freudian unconscious, the "knowledge which doesn't know itself," as Jacques Lacan used to say. If Rumsfeld thought that the main dangers in the confrontation with Iraq were the "unknown unknowns" – the threats from Saddam Hussein which we did not even suspect – what we should reply is that the main dangers are, on the contrary, the "unknown knowns," the disavowed beliefs and suppositions that we are not even aware that we ourselves hold. We could read Habermas's claim that we never knew so much about what we don't know through these four categories: the pandemic shook what we (thought we) knew that we knew; it made us aware of what we didn't know that we didn't know and; in the way we confronted it, we relied on what we didn't know that we knew (all our presumptions and prejudices which determine our acting, although we are not even aware of them). We are not dealing here with the simple transition from not-knowing to knowing but with the much more subtle transition from not-knowing to knowing what we don't know – in this transition our positive knowing remains the same, but we gain a free space for action.

It was with regard to the fourth category – what we didn't know that we knew – our presumptions and prejudices, that China (and Taiwan and Vietnam) did so much better than Europe and the United States in regard to the pandemic. I am getting tired of the oft-repeated objection: "Yes, the Chinese contained the virus, but at what price?" I agree that we need a Chinese Julian Assange to let us know what really went on there – the whole story – but the fact is that, when the epidemic exploded in Wuhan, they immediately imposed lockdown and brought the majority of production in the entire country to a standstill, clearly prioritizing human lives over the economy – with some delay, true, they took the crisis extremely seriously. Now they are reaping the reward, even in the economy. And – let's be clear – this was only possible because the Communist Party is still able to exert economic control and regulation: there is social control over market mechanisms, albeit a "totalitarian" one. But, again, the question is not how they did it in China but how should *we* do it. The Chinese way is not the only effective way; it is not "objectively necessary" in the sense that, if you analyse all the data, it can only be done in the

Chinese way. The epidemic is not just a viral process; it is a process that takes place within certain economic, social, and ideological coordinates that are open to change.

Now, as the twenty-first century moves forward, we live in a crazy time in which the hope that vaccines will work is met by a deepening depression, despair even, due to the growing number of infections and the almost daily discoveries of the new unknowns about the virus. In principle the answer to "What is to be done?" is easy here; we have the means and resources to restructure healthcare so that it serves the needs of the people in a time of crisis. However, to quote the last line of Bertolt Brecht's "In Praise of Communism" from his play *The Mother*: "It is the simple thing that is so hard to do."[7] There are many obstacles that make the simple thing hardest to do – above all the global capitalist order and its ideological hegemony. Do we then need a new communism? Yes, but what I am tempted to call a *moderately conservative communism*: all the steps that are necessary, from global mobilization against viral threats and other threats to establishing procedures that will constrain market mechanisms and socialize the economy, but undertaken in a way that is conservative (in the sense of an effort to conserve the conditions of human life – and the paradox is that we will have to change things precisely to maintain these conditions) and moderate (in the sense of carefully taking into account unpredictable side effects of our measures).

As Emmanuel Renault pointed out, the key marxian category that introduces class struggle into the very heart of the critique of political economy is that of so-called tendential laws, the laws that describe a necessary tendency in capitalist development, like the tendency of a falling profit rate. (As Renault noted, Theodor Adorno had already insisted on these dimensions of Marx's concept of *Tendenz* which make it irreducible to a simple "trend."[8]) Describing this "tendency," Marx himself uses the term *antagonism*: the falling rate of profit is a tendency that encourages capitalists to heighten the exploitation of workers, and pushes workers to resist it, so that the outcome is not predetermined but depends on the struggle – in some welfare states, organized workers have forced capitalists to make considerable concessions. The communism I am speaking about is exactly such a tendency: reasons for it are obvious (we need global action to fight health and environmental threats; the economy will have to be somehow socialized, for instance), and we should read the reactions of global capitalism to the pandemic precisely as *a set of reactions to the communist tendency*: the fake Great Reset, nationalist populism, solidarity reduced to empathy.

So how – if it does – will the communist tendency prevail? A sad answer: only through repeated crises. Let's be clear: the virus is atheist in the strongest sense of the term. Yes, we should analyse how the pandemic is socially conditioned, but it is basically a product of meaningless contingency; there is no "deeper message" in it (as they interpreted the plague as God's punishment in Medieval times). Before choosing Virgil's famous line, *acheronta movebo* ("I shall move the nether regions"), as the motto of his *Interpretation of Dreams*, Freud considered another candidate: Satan's words from Milton's *Paradise Lost*: "What reinforcement we may gain from Hope, / If not what resolution from despair." If we cannot be strengthened by hope, if we are compelled to admit that our situation is hopeless, we should gain resolve from despair. This is how we, contemporary Satans who are destroying our earth, should react to viral and ecological threats: rather than look vainly for strength in some hope, we should accept that our situation is desperate and act resolutely upon that acceptance.

To quote Greta Thunberg again: "Doing our best is no longer good enough. Now we need to do the seemingly impossible." Futurology deals with what is possible; we need to do what is (from the standpoint of the existing global order) *impossible*.

NOTES

1 "Existentielle Unsicherheit verbreitet sich jetzt global und gleichzeitig, und zwar in den Köpfen der medial vernetzten Individuen selbst"; "So viel Wissen über unser Nichtwissen und über den Zwang, unter Unsicherheit handeln und leben zu müssen, gab es noch nie." (Markus Schwering, "Jürgen Habermas on Corona: 'There has never been so much knowledge about our ignorance,'" *Frankfurter Rundschau,* 4 October 2020, https://www.fr.de/kultur/gesellschaft/juergen-habermas-coronavirus-krise-covid19-interview-13642491.html.)

2 RT *World News*, "Hungarian Cultural Commissioner Lights Powder Keg of Controversy after Describing Europe as 'George Soros' Gas Chamber,'" RT *World News*, 29 November 2020, https://www.rt.com/news/508146-soros-hungary-nazi-hitler-comparison/.

3 Suyin Haynes, "'We Now Need to Do the Impossible,' How Greta Thunberg Is Fighting for a Greener Post-Pandemic World," *Time,*

8 December 2020, https://time.com/5918448/greta-thunberg-coronavirus-climate-change/.

4 Jason Baer, "Coronavirus and the Great Reset," SYPartners, 3 April 2020, https://www.sypartners.com/insights/leading-unknown-coronavirus-great-reset/.

5 Adam Shapiro, "Capitalism 'Will Collapse on Itself' without More Empathy and Love: Scott Galloway," yahoo, 1 December 2020, https://www.yahoo.com/lifestyle/capitalism-will-collapse-on-itself-without-empathy-love-scott-galloway-120642769.html.

6 I have used this example many times in my work, most extensively in chapter 9 of In Defense of Lost Causes (London: Verso Books, 2017).

7 "Er ist das Einfache, das schwer zu machen ist."

8 See Theodor W. Adorno, Philosophische Elemente einer Theorie der Gesellschaft (Frankfurt: Suhrkamp, 2008), 37–40.

Contributors

CHIARA BOTTICI is a philosopher and critical theorist. She is director of gender studies and associate professor of philosophy at The New School. Her most recent books include *A Philosophy of Political Myth* (2007), *Imaginal Politics: Images beyond Imagination and the Imaginary* (2014), *Anarchafemminism* (2021), and *A Feminist Mythology* (2021). With sociologist Benoit Challand, she also co-authored *Imagining Europe: Myth, Memory, Identity* (2013) and *The Myth of the Clash of Civilizations* (2010). She also co-edited the collections of essays *The Politics of Imagination* (2011), *The Anarchist Turn* (2013), and *Feminism, Capitalism, and Critique* (2017). Her work has been translated into ten foreign languages and had an impact on the fields of philosophy, sociology, political science, and aesthetics.

ROSI BRAIDOTTI is distinguished university professor emerita at Utrecht University. She holds honorary degrees from Helsinki (2007) and Linkoping (2013); has been a fellow of the Australian Academy of the Humanities (FAHA) since 2009 and a member of the Academia Europaea (MAE) since 2014; and was the recipient of a Humboldt Research Award in 2022. Her main publications include *Nomadic Subjects* (1994 and 2011a) and *Nomadic Theory* (2011b), and *The Posthuman* (2013), *Posthuman Knowledge* (2019), and *Posthuman Feminism* (2022). In 2016 she co-edited *Conflicting Humanities* with Paul Gilroy; in 2018 *The Posthuman Glossary* with Maria Hlavajova, and in 2022 *More Posthuman Glossary*. Her interdisciplinary work has three main focal points: contemporary subjectivity, feminist theories, and the posthuman convergence.

CLEO DAVIS combines the disciplines of cultural and creative arts
to provide the African-American community with access to professional design and advocating for tools of economic growth and policy
change. Formally educated in architecture and industrial design, Davis
takes a critical view of social, political, and cultural issues, reproducing familiar visual signs and arranging them into new conceptually
layered pieces. As artist-in-residence at the City of Portland Archives,
Davis co-created, together with Kayin Talton-Davis, numerous public
art installations and projects such as the "Historic Black Williams Art
Project" and the "Alberta Street Black Heritage" markers. They co-
instructed an architectural studio at University of Oregon, centred on
developing concepts for the future ARTchive.

HENRY A. GIROUX currently holds the McMaster University Chair
for Scholarship in the Public Interest in the English and Cultural
Studies Department and is the Paulo Freire Distinguished Scholar in
Critical Pedagogy. His most recent books include *American
Nightmare: Facing the Challenge of Fascism* (2018), *The Terror of
the Unforeseen* (2019), *On Critical Pedagogy* (2nd edition, 2020),
Neoliberalism's War on Higher Education (2nd edition, 2020), *Race,
Politics, and Pandemic Pedagogy: Education in a Time of Crisis*
(2021), and *Pedagogy of Resistance: Against Manufactured Ignorance*
(2022). Giroux's latest book is *Insurrections: Education in the Age
of Counter-Revolutionary Politics* (forthcoming, 2023). He is also a
member of *Truthout*'s board of directors.

JENNIFER D. GRUBBS is an enviro-feminist anthropologist in the
Department of Anthropology at Antioch College. Prior to that
appointment she served as assistant director of the Women's Studies
Program and visiting assistant professor at East Tennessee State
University. She is the author of *Ecoliberation: Imagining Resistance
and the Green Scare* (2021). Grubbs has conducted ethnographic
work with environmental and animal advocacy movements based in
North America, with immigration-support communities in rural
Virginia, and with Holocaust survivors residing in Cincinnati, Ohio.

AMELIA JONES is Robert A. Day Professor and vice dean of faculty
and research at Roski School of Art & Design, USC, and a curator
and scholar of contemporary art, performance, and feminist/sexuality
studies. Recent publications include *Seeing Differently: A History and*

Theory of Identification and the Visual Arts (2012); *Otherwise: Imagining Queer Feminist Art Histories* (2016, co-edited with Erin Silver); and "On Trans/Performance," the edited special issue of *Performance Research* (2016). *Queer Communion: Ron Athey* (2020), Jones's catalogue co-edited with Andy Campbell, which accompanied a retrospective of Athey's work at Participant Inc. (New York) and ICA (Los Angeles), was listed among "Best Art Books 2020" in the *New York Times*. Her 2021 book, *In Between Subjects: A Critical Genealogy of Queer Performance*, explores the history of performance art and queer theory since the 1950s, from a queer feminist point of view.

KATERINA (KATARINA) KOLOZOVA is senior researcher and professor at the Institute of Social Sciences and Humanities, Skopje, and visiting faculty at Arizona State University Center for Philosophical Technologies. She teaches contemporary political philosophy at the Faculty of Media and Communications, Belgrade. She was a visiting scholar in the Department of Rhetoric at the University of California-Berkeley (2009) and a Columbia University NY-SIPA Visiting Scholar at its Paris Global Centre (2019). She sits on the board of directors of the New Centre for Research and Practice (Seattle, WA) and is a co-director of the School of Materialist Research (Tempe, AZ, Vienna, Eindhoven, Skopje). Kolozova is the author of *Cut of the Real: Subjectivity in Poststructuralist Philosophy* (2014) and *Capitalism's Holocaust of Animals: A Non-Marxist Critique of Capital, Philosophy and Patriarchy* (2019). Her numerous recent publications include an article in the issue on "Philosophy after Automation" of *Philosophy Today* (2021) and "Poststructuralism," a chapter in *The Oxford Handbook of Feminist Philosophy* (2021).

ALEX TAEK-GWANG LEE, philosopher and cultural critic, is professor of cultural studies at the School of Global Communication and a founding director of the Center for Technology in Humanities at Kyung Hee University, Korea. He has been visiting professor at the Centre for Culture Media and Governance, Jamia Millia Islamia University, India, and international visiting scholar at the Institute for Advanced Studies in Humanities and Social Sciences, National Taiwan University. He served as academic adviser for the Gwangju Biennale (2017) and program manager for the Venice Biennale of Architecture (2021). He is a board member of the International

Consortium of Critical Theory Programs (ICCTP) and the Asia Theories Network (ATN). He edited *The Idea of Communism* (vol. 3, 2016) and *Deleuze, Guattari and the Schizoanalysis of Postmedia* (2023). He has written articles for journals such as *Telos, Deleuze and Guattari Studies,* and *Philosophy Today,* and chapters in *Balibar/ Wallerstein's "Race, Nation, Class": Rereading a Dialogue for Our Times* (2018), *Back to the '30s? Recurring Crises of Capitalism, Liberalism, and Democracy* (2020), *The Bloomsbury Handbook of World Theory* (2021), and *Thinking with Animation* (2021).

NATASHA LENNARD is a contributing writer for *The Intercept,* and her work has appeared regularly in the *New York Times, The Nation, Esquire, Vice, Salon,* and the *New Inquiry,* among others. She teaches critical journalism at The New School for Social Research in New York and co-authored *Violence: Humans in Dark Times* (2018, with Brad Evans). Lennard is the author of *Being Numerous: Essays on Non-Fascist Life* (2019).

MICHAEL LOADENTHAL is a postdoctoral research fellow at the University of Cincinnati, the executive director of the Peace and Justice Studies Association, and the founder and executive director of the Prosecution Project. He has taught courses for Georgetown University, Miami University, George Mason University, University of Cincinnati, University of Malta's Mediterranean Academy of Diplomatic Studies, the DC Jail, and the Jessup Correctional Institution (a maximum-security men's prison). He has served as dean's fellow for Mason's School for Conflict Analysis and Resolution, practitioner-in-residence for Georgetown's Center for Social Justice, research fellow at the Hebrew Union College Center for the Study of Ethics and Contemporary Moral Problems, senior research associate for George Mason University's Better Evidence Project, research team leader for Princeton University's Bridging Divides Initiative, and contract-based security researcher and trainer working to defend and support social movements on four continents.

EDUARDO MENDIETA is professor of philosophy, Latina/o studies, and affiliated faculty at the School of International Affairs and the Bioethics Program at Penn State University. He is the author of *The Adventures of Transcendental Philosophy* (2002) and *Global*

Fragments: Globalizations, Latinamericanisms, and Critical Theory (2007). He is also co-editor, with Jonathan VanAntwerpen, of *The Power of Religion in the Public Sphere* (2011); with Craig Calhoun and Jonathan VanAntwerpen, of *Habermas and Religion* (2013); and with Amy Allen, of *From Alienation to Forms of Life: The Critical Theory of Rahel Jaeggi* (2018), *The Cambridge Habermas Lexicon* (2019), *Justification and Emancipation: The Critical Theory of Rainer Forst* (2019), *Decolonizing Ethics: The Critical Theory of Enrique Dussel* (2021), and *Power, Neoliberalism, and the Reinvention of Politics: The Critical Theory of Wendy Brown* (2022). He was the 2017 recipient of the Frantz Fanon Outstanding Achievement Prize.

FRANCESCO PALLANTE is full professor of constitutional law at the University of Turin and a member of the Italian Association of Constitutionalists (AIC). He is on the editorial board of Italian and foreign legal journals and participates in the Legal Council of the Italian General Confederation of Labour (CGIL). He is a columnist for the newspaper *il manifesto*. His research and writings centre around such topics as the validity foundation of constitutions, unwritten law, constitution-making processes, parliamentary representation, the connection between social rights and financial constraints, the contrast of social inequalities, and regional autonomy. Pallante has also published *Il neoistituzionalismo nel pensiero giuridico contemporaneo* (2008); *Lineamenti di Diritto costituzionale* (2014, with Gustavo Zagrebelsky and Valeria Marcenò); *Loro diranno, noi diciamo: Vademecum sulle riforme istituzionali* (2016, with Gustavo Zagrebelsky); *Per scelta o per destino: La Costituzione tra individuo e comunità* (2018); *Contro la democrazia diretta* (2020); and *Elogio delle tasse* (2021).

ADRIAN PARR is the dean of the College of Design at the University of Oregon and a senior fellow of the Design Futures Council. She served as a UNESCO chair for eight years. She is the author of numerous publications, the most recent being *The Wrath of Capital: Neoliberalism and Climate Change Politics* (2014), *Birth of a New Earth: The Radical Politics of Environmentalism* (2017), and *Earthlings: Imaginative Encounters with the Natural World* (2022). She has produced and co-directed (with Sean Hughes) two award-winning documentaries: *The Intimate Realities of Water* and *Thirsty & Drowning in America.*

Creator and innovator KAYIN TALTON-DAVIS's work centres around her passion for fusing art grounded in Black heritage and culture with graphic design, mechanical engineering, community building, and education. Known for her vibrant colour palettes and unique aesthetic, Talton-Davis founded Soapbox Theory™ in 2001, with the mission of "Cultivating Black Joy™." She is a current artist-in-residence at the City of Portland Archives, and co-artist (with Cleo Davis) of the "Historic Black Williams Art Project" and the "Alberta Street Black Heritage Markers." Her most recent permanent public installation, *We've Been Here*, highlighting Oregon Black women in the early 1900s, is located in the Portland Building.

THAÏSA WAY, FASLA, is director of Garden and Landscape Studies at Dumbarton Oaks, a Harvard University research institution, and professor emerita in the College of Built Environments, University of Washington. She was a Garden Club of America Fellow in Landscape Architecture at the American Academy in Rome in 2016 and the Mercedes Bass Visiting Scholar in 2023. She was founding director of Urban@UW, a cross-university initiative of the University of Washington. Way's book *Unbounded Practices: Women, Landscape Architecture in the Early Twentieth Century* (2009 and 2013) received the J.B. Jackson Book Award. Her *The Landscape Architecture of Richard Haag: From Modern Space to Urban Ecological Design* (2015) explores the narrative of post-industrial cities and practices of landscape architecture. Seeking to bring urban and environmental history into conversation, she edited *River Cities/City Rivers* (2018). She is currently co-editing (with Eric Avila) a volume of essays entitled *Segregation and Resistance in the Landscapes of the Americas* (forthcoming, 2023).

SANTIAGO ZABALA is ICREA (Catalan Institute for Research and Advanced Studies) Research Professor of Philosophy at the Pompeu Fabra University in Barcelona. He is the author of many books, including *Why Only Art Can Save Us: Aesthetics and the Absence of Emergency* (2017) and *Being at Large: Freedom in the Age of Alternative Facts* (2020). His opinion articles have appeared in the

New York Times, Al-Jazeera, and the *Los Angeles Review of Books,* among other international media outlets.

Slavoj Žižek is a Hegelian philosopher, a Lacanian psychoanalyst, and a communist. He is international director at the Birkbeck Institute for Humanities, University of London, U K; visiting professor at New York University, U S A; and senior researcher in the Department of Philosophy, University of Ljubljana, Slovenia. Žižek's latest book is *Surplus-Enjoyment: A Guide for the Non-Perplexed* (2022).

Index